rororo sprachen
Herausgegeben von Ludwig Moos

Unsere häufigsten Fehler im Englischen sind typisch deutsch. *Better Your English* behandelt die Fallen, in die wir Deutschen immer wieder tappen. Ob *false friends*, *grammatical mishaps* oder *cross-cultural faux pas* – hier werden die Tücken der englischen Sprache locker und praxisnah enttarnt. Pfiffige Übungen helfen, die unangenehmen Begleiter auf fremdem Sprachterrain ein für allemal loszuwerden.

Dr. René Bosewitz ist native speaker und leitet eine Sprachschule in Heidelberg. Zusammen mit Robert Kleinschroth hat er bei rororo sprachen *Joke Your Way Through English Grammar* (8527) und *Joke by Joke to Conversation* (8795) veröffentlicht, außerdem in der Reihe Business English *Manage in English* (60137), *Better than the Boss* (60138), *How to Phone Effectively* (60139), *Drop Them a Line* (60261, mit Bryan Hemming), *Test Your Management Skills* (60260), *Get Through at Meetings* (60262), *Let's Go International* (60267), *Check Your Language Level* (60268), *Business English from A to Z* (60269, mit Bryan Hemming), *The Way Things Work* (60369), *How to Read the Business Press* (60506), *Small Talk for Big Business* (60439) und *Business by Jokes* (60721), *Sell like Hell* (60722) und *Master Your Business Phrases* (60725).

René Bosewitz

Better Your English

Wie man typisch deutsche
Fehler verlernt

Rowohlt Taschenbuch Verlag

A special thanks to Anne Trumpfheller for her work and support.

Originalausgabe
Veröffentlicht im Rowohlt Taschenbuch Verlag GmbH,
Reinbek bei Hamburg, Oktober 1999
Copyright © 1999 by Rowohlt Taschenbuch Verlag GmbH,
Reinbek bei Hamburg
Umschlaggestaltung Büro Hamburg
(Illustration Gerd Huss)
Layout Anne Drude
Illustrationen Zarina Sheriff
Satz Stone Serif / Sans PostScript; QuarkXPress 3.32
Druck und Bindung Clausen & Bosse, Leck
Printed in Germany
ISBN 3 499 60802 2

The Contents

1	Lachnit at the Volkshochschule	7
2	Troublesome travelling	15
3	The host family	23
4	First day at the language course	29
5	At the pub	36
6	I'm lost	44
7	A game called cricket	51
8	An English rose	59
9	Going shopping	66
10	An apple a day keeps the doctor away	74
11	Off to bonny Scotland	81
12	Letting your hair down English style	88
13	Collecting culture	94
14	All good things must come to an end	102

	Appendix I: Extra idioms	109
	Appendix II: The right word at the right time	116
	Appendix III: Key to the exercises	122
	Appendix IV: Vocabulary	132

Foreword

So what is this book all about? Well, first you should enjoy it. It's light and humorous. Nobody is on the "test stand[1]". Next, it looks at some typical mistakes which arise because you have German as a native language. Speakers of other languages would make other types of mistakes.

These "false friends" have been built into light and typical dialogues. In these discussions we can follow Ernst Lachnit, our hero, as he jumps into English culture and typically English situations and meets island attitudes. He makes mistakes, and learns from them. In the footnotes you can find the way the "motherspeaker[2]" says it. There's a short, simple grammar overview in almost every chapter. The "culture corner" gives some insight into how Anglo-Saxons think and act. Some typical idioms spice up the chapters.

The book is rounded off by a quiz about the things we looked at with Ernst and his friends on their language trip through England. The appendix contains some extra interesting idioms. You might like to learn a few of them.

Although we are having a humorous look at Ernst's typically German sins, we should all keep in mind that nearly every one of us says some sort of "unsense[3]" when we speak a foreign language!

But keep on trying!!!

A last word to the title *Better Your English*. It's not quite right, not quite wrong. You can say "I want to better myself". It means "I want to do better in life, more money, more education etc.". In this meaning here it should read "Improve your English". So go ahead and "better your English".

---

1 Prüfstand = test bed or test rig → here: *this is no examination*
2 → *native speaker*
3 → *talk rubbish* or *make mistakes*

Lachnit at the Volkshochschule

Like many other people in the Federal Republic of Germany Ernst Lachnit visited[1] the gymnasium[2]. (He should have been another Arnold Schwarzenegger after 13 years, but see the footnote).
Then he became[3] a job at a local, but very successful engineering company. It could also have been a chemical company, car producer or bank. Ernst is a pretty typical case.
Suddenly the company where he worked began to fill up with foreigners. Not the sort selling pizzas and döners but decision-makers and managers. And they all spoke English. And then the hardest stroke[4] of all. English became the official company language.
Ernst decided it was time to act. He attended an intermediate course at the V.H.S. (In England this is called the adult education centre or evening school.) After three months he decided it was more a question of meeting a girl than learning English. Ernst managed to join a small group going for a quick "Pils" with his course tutor, Michael (Mick) Disney.

Mike: Where are you from, Ernst?
Ernst: Heidelberg.
Mike: Oh, nice, which part?
Ernst: All of me, Mr Disney.

---

1 Schule besuchen = *attend* school, *go to* school, not visit
2 Gymnasium = *grammar school (BrE), high school (AmE)*; Gymnasium in English is a sports hall!
3 become, became, become = werden ➔ *get, got, got* = bekommen
4 stroke = Hirnschlag oder Schlag bei einem Ballsport ➔ *blow* = Schicksalsschlag

Lachnit at the Volkshochschule

1 At O'Reilly's Irish Pub, Heidelberg

T = Terry (the owner of a pub); E = Ernst; V = Voices; M = Mick

(*Sound of glasses clinking*)

T: What can I be getting you gents? (He's from Ireland, that's why he uses the continuous form of the verb. Normally it's "what can I get you?").

E: I become[5] a pint of Guinness. But please, make you[6] it cold.

T: Sure, and it's always cold in the summer months. A pint of Guinness, then. And you other lads?

V: Okay, hmm!

T: So, it's Guinness all round then.

M: You know, Ernst, you get cold beer in England, too. You can also get it at room temperature during the winter. There are hundreds of different sorts.

E: Yes, I see. Thank you. But I must[7] be careful with my weight. I'm already too thick[8] from all this beer and sausage. Mike, I wanted to ask you something. I think I need to spend some time in England.

M: Oh, you mean you're tired of all the stress here. Well, I can understand that.

E: No, no, this was not my meaning.[9] Give you me[6] the name and address of a good school so that I can better[10] my English.

M: Right. I've got it. You want to do an intensive course in England for a couple of weeks. I know just the place. It's called Pilgrims. It's right down in the Southeast just near Dover. I'll get you a registration form and all the details.

E: I thank myself[11], Mick.

M: Simply say "thank you", Ernst.

E: Okay. Thank you, Ernst.

---

5 I become = ich werde → *I'll have* = ich bekomme
6 Befehlsform = make, do, speak, tell; hier: *make it cold* (not: make you it cold); *give me* (not: give you me)
7 I must = ich muß unbedingt – is very strong and hard. Normally we would say "*I have to*" → *I really have to leave now*
8 False friend: when talking about a person "thick" means stupid. (You can have a thick book but a person is "*fat*".)
9 meaning = Bedeutung. → Meinung = *opinion*
10 → *improve*. "Better" is used with self in "better oneself financially."
11 → *thank you very much*

Lachnit at the Volkshochschule

❗ Trouble-shoot that English

The Imperative (Befehlsform) in English is a little different from the German. Look at the following tip and say goodbye to your mistakes.

Wrong	Right
Make you the beer cold!	Make the beer cold, please!
Sign you the registration form!	Sign the registration form, please!

TIP 1

Simply take the infinitive of the verb. Put "please" at the end and eliminate the "you".

Speak a little slower, please.
Drive carefully, please.

TIP 2

You can be more polite if you say:

Could you speak a little slower, please?
Could you sign the registration form, please?

If you want to tell somebody not to do something, say:

Don't speak too loudly, please.
Don't leave the pub without paying.
Do not argue with me all the time.

In an English pub

Customer: Could you give me something long, cold and half full of vodka?
Barman: How about my wife?

Lachnit at the Volkshochschule

1. Culture-crossing ▷ Ireland

Ernst's first contact with the English-speaking world was in the Irish pub, O'Reilly's. Pubs are an important part of life all over Britain and Ireland. You should know that they're a bit different from *Wirts-* and *Gasthäuser* in *Germania*.

Opening times
Typical pubs open at 11 in the morning. Some stay open the whole day and close at approximately 11 o'clock in the evening.

Social life
Pubs in Ireland are places to go to meet people. So customers often stand around in small groups near the bar. Talking to strangers is quite normal. The Irish will discuss anything with you from the political situation in Europe or at home, through rugby to the weather. They'll even talk about the qualities of their black gold – no, not oil, they haven't really got any, I mean the Guinness. You'll certainly notice that many Irish have the gift of the gab. This basically means that they are able to speak fluently on almost every topic (although it may not be their real opinion about the matter and might even be nonsense). They sound very eloquent.

Customs
In typical pubs you shouldn't expect to sit around a table and be your own private little group. That reminds me of a story which took place in Cork one Saturday morning. A German gentleman and his wife came into a pub, sat down at one of the tables and waited for the barman to come to serve them, which, of course, he did not. After ten minutes the German couple left cursing the Irish for their bad service. You see, you have to go to the bar to order. No one will come to your table. On the other hand, when I first came to Germany I often went up to the bar to order something and was mostly sent off with a flea in my ear. They thought "rude foreigner, pushing to the front", and I thought, well, you can guess what I thought. Back to Ireland; in many pubs you can find a warm buffet on the bar. You should serve yourself. Of course, there are pubs and "pubby" restaurants where you have waitress service. Keep your eyes open and don't expect things to be like they are at home.

Lachnit at the Volkshochschule

Drinking

There is a whole range of drinks. Traditionally people (especially the men) drink Guinness (a black, heavy, bitter ale) or Beamish (a lighter version) or lager beer (ice cold and something like a form of export but not so sweet). They speak for themselves. That reminds me of a story about my friend O'Shanahan from Dublin. He went into a pub and ordered 17 pints of Guinness. When the barman gave them to him he placed them in a line and then hastily swallowed down the first pint, then the third, then the fifth, seventh, ninth, eleventh, fifteenth and seventeenth. He wiped his mouth and got up to leave.

"Don't you want the other drinks?" asked the barman.

"No, thanks," replied O'Shanahan. "My doctor said I could only have the odd drink ..." (odd = gelegentlich. When talking about figures it also means "ungerade".)

Now it's your turn

1. Look at the following dialogue.

Ernst is speaking "Lachnitisches" English. Can you "better" his English? Answers are in the Key to the exercises.

R = Receptionist; **E** = Ernst (on the phone)

R: Hello, Pilgrims speaking. Kathy here. How can I help you?
E: Hallo, Ernst Lachnit at the apparat. Speak you please louder. I can you accoustish not hear.
R: I'm sorry. There seems to be some interference on the line.
E: Yes, I think also that we have a bad cable. My dame, I wish to register me in your English course in July.
R: Do you want to register for one of our English language courses?
E: Naturally. This is why I call you. Send you once a formula to me and I fill it out.
R: Okay. I think you want me to send you our enrolment form. Could you tell me your address, please?
E: The faster, the better. Send you, please, the formulas per fax. I will begin July 10.
R: Okay. Don't worry. I'll fax them to you immediately.
E: I thank myself. Cheers!

Lachnit at the Volkshochschule

2. What would a native speaker say for the following?

a) Ich besuchte das Gymnasium dreizehn Jahre lang, und dann wurde ich Polizist.
b) Es gelang mir, einen Platz in einem Sprachkurs zu bekommen.
c) Ich habe das Vergnügen, dieses Buch zu lesen, um mein Englisch zu verbessern.

3. Which of the following sentences is best?

a) Decide what your level of English is and tick (✓) the box. ❑
Decide what your level of English is and tick you the box. ❑
Decide what your level of English is and could you tick the box? ❑

b) Don't send you off the registration form until you've signed it. ❑
Not send off the registration form until you've signed it. ❑
Don't send off the registration form until you've signed it. ❑

c) I've eaten too much today. I feel as thick as hell. ❑
I've eaten too much today. I feel as fat as hell. ❑
I've eaten too much today. I feel as large as hell. ❑

d) All the beer in England is warm? That wasn't my meaning. ❑
All the beer in England is warm? I didn't want to say that. ❑
All the beer in England is warm? I wanted not to say that. ❑

4. General Great Britain and Ireland Quiz

1. What's the capital of the Republic of Ireland?
   a) Belfast   b) Cork   c) Dublin

2. Where are Celtic languages spoken in the British Isles?

3. Where did the game of golf originate?
   a) Ireland   b) England   c) Scotland

4. Approximately how many litres is a pint?
   a) 0.4   b) 0.6   c) 1.6

Lachnit at the Volkshochschule

5. What's the "average" price of a pub meal in Ireland?
   Example: steak, potatoes, vegetables or pie, chips and veg.
   a) £5 – £7   **b)** £7 – £10   **c)** £3 – £5

6. Which is an Irish whisky?
   a) Glen Fiddach   **b)** Jamesons   **c)** Jack Daniels

7. Where was the game of rugby invented?
   a) Ireland   **b)** Scotland   **c)** England

8. Which two of the following are Irish national dishes?
   a) Guinness + oysters   **b)** Steak and kidney pie
   c) Shepherd's pie   **d)** Irish stew

Just a few idioms to lighten your life

German	Wrong	Right
Willst du mich durch den Kakao ziehen?	Do you want to pull me through the cocoa?	Are you pulling my leg?

Lachnit at the Volkshochschule

1

German	Wrong	Right
Sie hat nicht alle Tassen im Schrank.	She hasn't got all her cups in the cupboard.	She's a bit nutty. She's got bats in the belfry.

Troublesome travelling

Ernst filled in all his forms correctly and got onto a course of English at Pilgrims, Canterbury. He booked a ticket with British Airwegs (BA, some say it stands for "bloody awful") to Heathrow in London.

He has just arrived in England and is sitting in one of the lounges at the airport waiting for his luggage to arrive. There has been a problem. In the seat next to him is a young lady. But first read these jokes.

Telephoning for information about schedules

Ernst: Is that British Airwegs? Can you tell me how long it takes to fly from Frankfurt to London?
Clerk: Just a minute, sir ...
Ernst: Okay. Thanks a lot. Goodbye.

The bearded man stuck a gun in the pilot's back and hissed: "Take me to London!"
Pilot: "But we're supposed to be going to London anyway!"
Bearded man: "I know. But I've been hi-jacked to Cuba twice before so this time I'm taking no chances!"

Troublesome travelling

2 → Losing luggage

E = Ernst; A = Amy; C = Clerk; CO = Customs officer

E: Well, this is typical. You can never trust these airlines. They're often losing¹ things.

A: I beg your pardon. What did you say? Who's losing what?

E: I talk about¹ British Airwegs. I'm reading⁽¹⁾ about it every day that they are losing luggages². They are all so busy they have no oversight³.

A: Oh right. I know what you mean. And I've got to work over here for two months, so I need my luggage.

E: Also⁴, you do not normally live in England, Miss eh ...?

A: Amy, Amy Frandango. No, most of the year I work in Heidelberg in Germany. I'm an English teacher.

E: You're teaching¹ in Germany, in Heidelberg? That's my hometown, too. And now I'm travelling to Canterbury for my English course at Pilgrims.

A: What a coincidence! I'm going to Canterbury as well to teach at Pilgrims.

E: Perhaps you will be my teacher. Very good, please let me spend⁵ you a cup of coffee. Then we can go to the baggage claim to see if our cases have arrived.

(Half an hour later at the baggage claim office)

E: Hello. My luggage has not arrived. It has disappeared. Please find my cases.

C: Now calm down, sir. We'll do our best. Now, which flight was it?

E: British Airwegs. Number 654. It arrived at 15.40 today.

C: Okay. If you'd be so kind as to fill in this form. Name, address, destination etc.

---

1 Wrong verb system. We have Present Simple (action repeats itself every day, every hour, often) and Present Continuous (action is going on NOW).
He is speaking very loudly at the moment. (NOW) = Present Continuous
→ *They often lose things* = Simple Present
2 Luggage has no plural form. You can say "*2 pieces of luggage*" or "*I have some luggage*". It is the same with baggage.
3 oversight = Versehen → *overview, bird's eye view* = Übersicht, Überblick
4 German "also" → "*so*" in English. The English word "also" means "auch"
5 spend = Geld ausgeben → "Please let me *invite/ treat you* to a cup of coffee"

Troublesome travelling

(Half an hour later, Ernst and Amy passing through customs)
CO: Thank you, madam. Sir, could I just see your passport, please?
E: Pass[6] again? Everybody wants my documents, but nobody finds my cases. Now I have the salad[7]. Please[8].
CO: You're travelling very light, sir. May I ask where you're going, the purpose of your visit and how long you'll be staying in the UK? Haven't you got any suitcases?
E: Yes, I have suitcases, or I mean I had. They haven't arrived.

❗ Trouble-shoot that English

Wrong	Right
I'm reading about it every day.	I read about it every day.
I talk about British Airwegs.	I'm talking about British Airwegs.

This is a favourite mistake amongst Germans. In English we have two types of Present Tense, two types of Past Tense etc. The Simple forms and the Continuous (Progressive) ones. Tidy up your Present Tenses by reading on.

(**TIP**)

Verb Systems

Present Continuous	Present Simple
She's doing it NOW	*She does it REGULARLY*
The action is happening NOW, it is continuing.	This action repeats itself
He is shouting at the moment.	*He shouts every time he sees her.*
They are drinking wine now.	*They often drink beer or water.*

---

6 Pass = vorbeigehen → *passport* = Paß
7 The construction "Now I have the salad" (jetzt habe ich den Salat) is not possible → *Now I'm in a mess*
8 When you pass something to somebody → *here you are*

Troublesome travelling

2

How to form a question

Are you signing this form now?   *Do you often sign such stupid documents?*

Is he watching TV at the moment?   *Does he often watch this sort of film?*

Ernst: A return ticket, please.
Airline reservation clerk: Where to, sir?
Ernst: Back here, please.

The air stewardess was being interviewed by her boss:
"Tell me, what would you do if you found yourself in a dive?"
Air stewardess: "I'd drink up quickly and get out."

✱ Extra information   ▷ English language schools

Read on and you'll get an idea what might await you on an English language course. Look at the following excerpt of a brochure from a language school in England:

> - This course is designed for all those who wish to concentrate on improving their English.
> - The course consists of 15 hours of class tuition per week and is taught in small groups, max. 12 persons.
> - A level placement test, consisting of grammar and listening components, is given in the first session of the course, and students are allocated to a group of the appropriate level.
> - Participants follow course books. To reinforce learning, role-plays, video and audio activities are included.

A typical course timetable looks like this:

	9:00 – 10:30	11:00 – 12:30	13:30 – 15:00	
Monday	Introductory activities	Speaking – Discussion about feelings	Pairwork Design a house	HOMEWORK
	Prepositions	Language feedback	Role-play	
Tuesday	Vocabulary building	Listening work: BBC News	Video on business meetings	HOMEWORK
	Exercises	Exercises	Exercises	

Troublesome travelling

Interested? Well, if you want to register for a language course in England you have to fill out a registration form. Every school uses its own form, but the following example might make it a little bit easier for you to fill out your own.

Personal details:
Family Name: _Lachnit_   Male or Female? _male_
First Names: _Ernst_
Nationality: _German_   Age: _30_   Date of Birth: _3 / 4 / 69_
Address: _2 Belfortstrasse_
69115 Heidelberg

Telephone No: _06221 145321_   Fax: __
Passport Number: _D 16245 E_
Emergency Contact Name: _Jasmine Lachnit_   Relationship: _mother_
Telephone/Fax: __
How did you hear about us? _in the VHS_

Course details:
Type of course: _intensive_
Number of lessons per week: ~~three~~ _twenty_
Course Dates: From _July 1st 1999_ to _July 29_   Number of Weeks: _3_
Level of English: _intermediate_
Other languages spoken: _no_

Travel details (If Known):
Arrival: Airport/port ____ Date: ____ Time: ____ Flight No ____
Departure: Airport/port ____ Date: ____ Time: ____ Flight No: ____
I will send them later

Accommodation: (please tick the boxes to show the type of accommodation)
I will arrange my own accommodation ☐
Type of Accommodation required: Host Family ☒   Single☐   Shared ☐   Executive☐
B & B ☐   Hostel ☐   Hotel ☐
Hotel only: What Grade? *☐ **☐ ***☐ ****☐
Do you smoke Yes ☒ No☐
Do you have any allergies or illnesses: _no_
Do you have any special diets (e.g. vegetarian)? _I like lots of meat_
Any other special requirements about your course or accommodation?
running water

I agree to the conditions in the brochure, and will pay all course fees due. I enclose a registration fee of £50 which I understand is non-returnable.

Signed: _Ernst Lachnitt_   Date: _June 1th 1999_

Troublesome travelling

At the language school

Teacher: Ernst, give me a sentence beginning with "I".

Ernst: I is ...

Teacher (angrily): Ernst! How many more times do I have to tell you? You must always say "I am"!

Ernst: Okay, sir. I am the letter in the alphabet after H.

Air traffic controller: What is your height and position?

Pilot: I'm about five feet ten inches tall and I'm sitting in the pilot's seat.

 Now it's your turn

1. Can you correct the lachnitische English in the following dialogue?

E = Ernst; **W** = Waiter; **C** = Chef

E: Mr Over, Mr Over. I will speak the cook.

W: Certainly, sir.

C: You summoned me, sir.

E: And whether I've done that. This steak and kidney pie is hard as stone. And it tastes horribly!

C: But my steak and kidney pies are delicious. I've been making them since before you were born.

E: But why must you serve them only now?

Troublesome travelling

2. Put the verbs in brackets into the correct form

It was one o'clock in the morning and the manager of the hotel had just been woken up by a frantic phone call from a little old lady.
"(Come) quickly! Oh, please (come) quickly," she cried.
"I can see a naked man from my window."
The manager dressed and rushed up to the little old lady's room. She (look) through the window and (point). All the manager could see was the top half of a man. "But madam," explained the manager, "the man only (prepare) for bed. And he may not be completely naked."
"The drawers", shrieked the little old lady. "(stand) on the drawers".

3. Which of the following sentences is best?

a. How many luggages do you have, sir?
   How many pieces of luggages do you have, sir?
   How much luggage do you have, sir?

b. I oversaw the fact that my bank card was out of date.
   I overlooked the fact that my bank card was out of date.
   I overviewed the fact that my bank card was out of date.

c. The police have stopped us. Now we're in a real mass.
   The police have stopped us. Now we have the salad.
   The police have stopped us. Now we're in a real mess.

4. Can you translate these simple sentences into English?

a. Ich möchte dir ein Bier spendieren.
b. Jim: Kannst du mir den Ketchup reichen?
   Ann: Bitte schön.
c. Ann: Meine Beine tun mir weh. Ich bin über eine Stunde gejoggt.
   Mutter: Also du solltest nicht übertreiben.

Troublesome travelling

2 Knock a few idioms into your head!

German	Wrong	Right
Um den heißen Brei herumreden.	To talk around the hot porridge.	To beat around the bush.

German	Wrong	Right
Du gehst mir auf den Keks.	You go me on the biscuit.	You're getting on my nerves.
Du hast einen Vogel.	You have a bird.	You're off your head.

The host family

So Ernst finally found his luggage. Then, together with Amy, he caught the train down to Canterbury East. Amy then left him to go to the University of Kent where she had a room. Ernst phoned his host family. Mr Woodcock arrived at the railway station ten minutes later.

Joy: I've just read an interesting article. It said that most accidents that happen, happen in the kitchen.
John: I know and you always expect me to eat them.

First impressions

E = Ernst; Jo = John; J = Joy

Jo: Hi, my name's John Woodcock. I think you might be waiting for me. (*Ernst shaking Mr Woodcock's hand firmly and for too long*).
E: Yes, how do you do? May I introduce myself? I am called Ernst Lachnit[1].
Jo: Welcome to England. By the way I hope you had a comfortable flight. How long did it take?
E: Yes, the airplane has taken[2] more than one hour.
Jo: And I believe you'll be staying for three weeks. It's a short time to master a language.
E: Yes, but my chef[3] would not give me free[4] from work for longer.
Jo: Never mind! Here's the car. Let's drive home and you can meet my wife.

---

1 A good way to introduce yourself is *"Hello, my name's Ernst Lachnit"*. "I'm called E.L." isn't natural English.
2 Ernst confuses Present Perfect with Simple Past ("has taken" with → *took*). General rule:
   Present Perfect – action finished but we don't know when – no time info
   Simple Past – action finished, we know when it finished
   Present Perfect – *I have visited Japan* (irgendwann mal)
   Simple Past – *I visited Japan last year* (time given)
3 English "chef" means "Koch". → Chef = *boss* or *chief*
4 "Give me free" is not English. → freigeben = *release* or *give me time off work*

The host family

3

(*10 minutes later*)

J: Hello, welcome to Canterbury. (*shakes hands with Ernst*)
E: How do you do? I'm called Ernst[1].
J: Where've you come from exactly?
E: I came[2] from Heidelberg in Germany. I've started[2] my journey at 2 p.m.
J: Right. Well, just sit down over there on the sofa and I'll make you a cup of tea, or would you prefer something stronger?
E: Oh, yes please. Something stronger. A cup of coffee.
J: No, you didn't understand me. I meant a small glass of whisky. Something to warm you up.
E: What a good idea! Perhaps that can help me to overwind[5] the problems I have had[2] at the airport.
J: So we could have our evening meal at about six-thirty if that's alright with you.
E: That's fine! I finish my course at 5 p.m. so I will have time to change my hose[6].
Jo: Is that a rubber hose, some sort of special equipment? Perhaps I can be of help?
E: No, no it's not necessary. They are in my suitcase in the floor[7].
J: Oh, I get it. You two are talking at cross-purposes. Ernst means his trousers, not a hose. Ernst, a hose is a rubber tube, a pipe.
Jo: Pipe. But not the one you put in your mouth!
E: Oh dear. Now I'm fully through one another[8].

❗ Trouble-shoot that English

Wrong	Right
I have driven the car yesterday.	I drove the car yesterday.
Yes, I have eaten curry when I was in India.	Yes, I ate curry when I was in India.

---

5 overwind = überdrehen (eine Uhr) → überwinden = *get over a problem*
6 hose = Schlauch → Hose = *trousers*
7 floor = Fußboden → Flur = *passage or hallway*
8 völlig durcheinander = confused, mixed up → *I'm really mixed up*

The host family

As you saw Ernst was confused about when to use Simple Past and Present Perfect. This is a common mistake made by German speakers. Here's a little hint.

TIP

Verb Systems

Simple Past	Present Perfect
He **left** the party 2 hours ago.	He **has left** the party.
Action finished – time information given about when it finished.	Action finished – no time info.

Typical phrases with Simple Past:

yesterday, two weeks ago, last winter, in the past etc.

Typical phrases with Present Perfect:

recently	=	neulich
already	=	schon
ever	=	jemals
never	=	niemals
yet	=	noch
not yet	=	noch nicht
for/since	=	seit

Ortrud: *Have* you *heard* the latest Clinton joke?   = Present Perfect
Rene: Yes, I *heard* it on the TV on last   = Simple Past
       night's news. "Clinton works well in
       the Oral Room."

Joy: And how did you find the steak then, Ernst?
Ernst: Oh, I just lifted up a chip and there it was.

The host family

René: Alex, could I have some undercooked chips, some rotten cold beans and a fried egg lying in old fat?
Alex: Of course not, René. I couldn't possibly give you anthing like that.
René: Why not? That's what you gave me yesterday.

Culture-crossing ▷ A few tips for spending time with English families

Eating

What time does dinner usually begin? Normally between eight and nine o'clock. Maybe a family will fix dinner earlier at seven o'clock. Dinner might begin half an hour later. Don't arrive too early, probably your hosts will be "caught with their trousers down" (see "Knock a few idioms into your head!" at the end of this chapter). That means they are doing everything at the last minute. If you're going to be late, give your hosts a quick phone-call.

Being helpful

At dinner you could offer to help your host, but you shouldn't do more than pour a few drinks, clear the table or carry a few dishes. Don't try to rush off and wash the pots. Your host will be embarrassed. You'll kill the relaxed atmosphere.

A few do's and don'ts at table

- Begin to eat as soon as you're ready. If you feel uncomfortable about that, wait for your neighbour to start. Make your hostess a compliment about the food. It's good for the ego.
- Back to our childhood. Don't talk with your mouth full. Nobody wants to monitor your half-masticated food, even if you're the greatest small-talker in the world.
- Don't wave your fork while talking. You're not a Viking.
- Don't put your elbows on the table. It doesn't belong to you.
- Don't stretch across your neighbour to get the salt. It's not the time for making love.

The host family

- Finally, don't linger or wait around until the early hours of the morning, especially if your hostess is speaking in words of one syllable between yawns. Remember all these things and you'll be a welcome guest.

Now it's your turn

1. The same old problem!

Repair our Ernst's English in the following joke:

In the bookshop
E = Ernst; **BA** = Bookshop assistant

E: I'd like to buy a roman, please.
BA: Certainly, sir. Do you have the title or name of the author?
E: Really not. I had hoped you could something suitable suggest that I could read.
BA: No problem. Do you like light or heavy reading?
E: That is me equal. I have the wagon straight for the shop.

2. Put the verbs (in brackets) in the correct form

The TV company (decide) to make a programme about successful executives, so they (call) five of them into the studio to talk about their lives and how they (manage) to be so successful.
The first four all (tell) about how they had fought to get to the top – all four of them (marry) their boss's daughters. But the fifth executive had had a really hard fight to become successful.
"Life (be) never easy for me. I (must) to fight for everything and times (be) often difficult. But I just (grit) my teeth, (roll) up my sleeves – and (get) down to asking Dad to lend me another £500,000."

3. Which of the following sentences is best?

a. How do you do? I'm called Amy Fandango. I'm your new teacher.
   Hi, my name's Amy Fandango. I'm your new teacher.
   Hello. I am Amy Fandango. I'm your new teacher.

The host family

3

b. I'm very impressed with this meal. Could I meet the cooker?
I'm very impressed with this meal. Could I meet the chief?
I'm very impressed with this meal. Could I meet the chef?

Get a few idioms into your head!

German	Wrong	Right
Ich mach mich auf die Socken.	I make myself on the socks.	I have to get going.
Er hat etwas auf dem Kasten.	He has something on the box.	He's brainy.
Wenn schon, denn schon.	When already, then already.	In for a penny, in for a pound.
Er wurde kalt erwischt.	He was caught cold.	He was caught with his trousers down.

First day at the language course

It's Monday morning, the first day at the English course. Ernst was taken by taxi to the centre where he and five other participants are getting their 9 o'clock briefing from the director of studies. Ernst is a little nervous. He remembers his old school days, all those marks and tests. And, most important, he doesn't want to lose face. "I hope I'm better than the others. At least I don't want to blame myself[1]." He notices that the other five are all professional people, too. At least two of them are managers. They look very well organised.

Secretary: Excuse me, sir, I think you're wanted on the phone.
Ernst: What do you mean "you think" I'm wanted on the phone? Either I am or I'm not!
Secretary: Well, sir, the caller asked if that stupid old idiot was in yet.

The manager called his assistant into his office and closed the door sternly. "Now listen to me", he said. "There's £50 missing from the petty cash box. There are only two keys to that box. I have one and you have the other." "Well", said the assistant, "suppose we each put in £25 and say no more about it!"

---

[1] to blame oneself = sich die Schuld geben → sich blamieren = *make a fool of oneself*

First day at the language course

4 → Back to school

Robert Fields is making a welcome briefing. Sitting in front of him are Ernst, Anna (from Italy), Jan (Denmark), Conchita (Portugal), Pyotr (Russia).

R = Rob; **E** = Ernst; **A** = Anna

R: ...and I know for some of you this is your first time in a seminar of this kind. Okay, that's all I wanted to say formally. Now, if any of you have any questions to ask, please feel free.

E: Thank you. Yes. I would like some informations[2] about the map[3] you have given us.

R: Map? Oh, you mean the street guide of Canterbury. Yes, what's the problem?

E: No, no, no!

A: Rob. I think he is talking about our folder with the general information in it.

E: Naturally[4]. Can you explain us[5] how a typical day will look like[6]?

R: You mean "what a typical day will look like"? And that's the first point. Your teachers will correct most of the mistakes they hear. Perhaps you should put ten pence in our mistake box for every mistake. Ha, ha.

E: My meaning[7] is you will become millionaires in a week. That might be a receipt[8] for getting rich, but I don't know if we'll learn a lot.

R: Your training begins every day at 9 o'clock. You work on structures of English, that's a modern way of saying grammar. Then at 11 o'clock there's vocabulary training, especially business English. In the afternoon we have presentations and role-plays.

A: Oh good! I like listening to presentations.

---

2 Some words in English have no plural with "s". *Information, data, furniture, advice, progress, etc.* → "*We have no information; she has a lot of furniture.*"
3 map = Landkarte → Mappe = *folder*
4 naturally = auf die natürliche Art und Weise → natürlich = *of course*
5 "Explain" is used with "to" → *Can you explain to us ...?*
6 "How it locks like" is wrong. → wie es aussieht = *what it looks like*
7 meaning = Bedeutung → meine Meinung = *my opinion*
8 receipt = Quittung → Kochrezept = *recipe*

First day at the language course

R: Perhaps I should clear up any misunderstandings. You, the students, prepare and make the presentation in English.
E: Oh, you dear time[9]! Isn't that overdriving[10]? I haven't spoken English since I was at school.
A: Don't get nervous, Ernst. You'll succeed. It'll be funny.
E: On side[11] two in the folder there stands[12] information about lunch.
R: That's right. You all go to lunch with your tutors. You have a pub meal together so you can continue to practise your English. Now, I think that's the most important stuff. Here are your timetables. Let's move over to the classroom.
E: Presentations in English. Role-plays. That knocks me over[13]. It's really like school. Ah, that reminds me. Anna, I know a joke about English.
A: Go on.
E: So the English teacher asked little Anna "What is the future of 'he drinks'?"
A: He will drink?
E: No, "he will be drunk", of course. Ha. Ha.
A: Oh my god. Is that a funny joke for you, Ernst?

Don't waste your time looking for grammar tips! There aren't any. Ernst had a good day, so he must have learned a lot of grammar at his language course.

Culture-crossing ▷ All about England

Football

The most popular spectator sport in England is football. English football clubs offer exciting entertainment. They have also won a lot of cups internationally. The same cannot be said of the English national team.

....

9 Lachnitsches English → ach du liebe Zeit! = *my goodness* or *my God* or *Jesus Christ!*
10 → übertreiben = *exaggerate*
11 → (Buch-)Seite = *page. On page two ...*
12 → es steht in der Zeitung/Brief → *it's written in the newspaper/letter*
   Here: *in the folder information is written about lunch*
13 Falsches Idiom. → das haut mich um = *that bowled me over. I was really shocked*

First day at the language course

4

A FEW QUOTES

"He's very fast and if he gets a yard ahead of himself nobody will catch him."
Bobby Robson

"An inch or two either side of the post and that would have been a goal."
Dave Basselt

"If history is going to repeat itself, I should think we can expect the same thing again."
Terry Venables

Nonsense

Sometimes the English have problems being accurate. Look at the following signs found in England. Do you notice anything strange?

Dinner Special

Turkey £ 2.35
Chicken or Beef £ 2.25
Children £ 2

For sale

Antique dresser suitable for lady with thick legs and large drawers

From time to time English people have to write to the authorities. Here are some parts of actual letters. Do you notice anything?

"I am pleased to inform you that my husband who was reported missing, is dead."

"In accordance with your instructions, I have given birth to twins in the enclosed envelope."

Say it the nice way

Of course the English never say anything directly. They tend to "beat around the bush" (talk around the hot porridge). Read on till you get the message.

First day at the language course

- He does not get falling-down drunk;
  he becomes accidentally horizontal.
- He is not a sex machine;
  he is romantically automated.
- He does not have a beer gut;
  he has a liquid grain storage facility.

So much for the English!

Now it's your turn

1. Can you help poor old struggling Ernst?

In a pub in Canterbury. It is 14:35. Some pubs close for the afternoon. Ernst tries to order a beer. **E** = Ernst; **B** = Barmaid

E: Hello, girl, can you me a beer give?
B: I beg your pardon. Are you speaking to me?
E: Naturally. I have thirst. Tap me a fresh beer, please.
B: What do you mean "a fresh beer"? What do you want?
E: For the sake of God. I need "pils" from the barrel.
B: I think you need a doctor. Anyway, you're out of luck.
We closed five minutes ago.
E: Police hour? I thought this be a democracy.

2. A little spontaneous practice

Put the words in brackets in the correct form:

Amy (love) her elderly grandmother dearly and (decide) that for Christmas she would buy her a parrot as it would be someone for her to talk to and keep her company.
Amy (go) to a pet shop and (insist) that the parrot had to have a large vocabulary. She (pay) a thousand pounds for the most talkative parrot ever. Amy (arrange) for the parrot to be delivered to her grandma on Christmas Eve.
"How you (like) the bird I sent you?"
"It (be) delicious!" she replied.

First day at the language course

3. Which is the best?

a. I explained him the problem before he tried.
   I explained the problem to him before he tried.
   I explained to him the problem before he tried.

b. To make a really good paella I really need the ....
   receipt
   recipe
   quitting.

c. Don't ....! You didn't run 100 metres in ten seconds.
   overdrive
   drive over
   exaggerate

4. Put it into good English!

a. Guck mal her. Es steht auf Seite fünfzehn.
b. In der Apotheke: "Geben Sie mir bitte eine Quittung für die Medikamente."
c. Meiner Meinung nach sollten wir alle kein Fleisch mehr essen.

"Hello", said the school teacher, answering the phone.
"This is Miss Cotton of class three at Spondon Secondary School".
"Hello", said the voice on the phone. "I'm phoning to tell you that Johnny Brown is sick and won't be coming to school today."
"Oh, I am sorry to hear that", commented the teacher.
"Who is that speaking?"
The voice on the telephone replied: "This is my father."

"Help, help!" shouted the man in the sea. "I can't swim."
"So what?" shouted back a drunk from the shore. "I can't play the piano, but I'm not shouting about."

First day at the language course

🌀 Would you believe it – more idioms

4

German	Wrong	Right
Einen neuen Anfang machen.	Make a new beginning.	Turn over a new leaf.
Jemanden hinters Licht führen.	Lead somebody behind the lights.	Pull the wool over somebody's eyes.
Das ist ein starkes Stück.	That's a strong piece.	What a cheek! That's going too far.
Ich habe Gänsehaut.	I've got goose skin.	I've got goose pimples.
Jemanden für dumm verkaufen.	Sell someone for foolish.	Think someone is stupid.

At the pub

5

The first day at the school went quite well for Ernst, although he felt tired. He wasn't used to speaking English all day long. Fortunately he wasn't worse than the rest. "At least I haven't lost my[1] face." After school he was taken to his host family. There was no dinner that night because all the course participants wanted to meet to go to an old pub in the countryside. Kathy, responsible for leisure activities was to accompany them.

The drunk came tottering out of a pub and found a man selling tortoises.
"How much are they?" asked the drunk.
"Only ten pounds each", replied the man.
"I'll take one", said the drunk, and after he had paid for the tortoise he took it and staggered off. After twenty minutes the drunk came swaying up to the tortoise seller and bought another tortoise before staggering off again.
Fifteen minutes later the drunk returned to the tortoise seller.
"You know", he said as he bought another tortoise, "they're very expensive – but by Jove, I really love your crunchy pies."

At the pub

(*The group is standing near the bar*).

K = Kathy; **A** = Anna; **C** = Conchita; **E** = Ernst; **B** = Barmaid; **J** = Jan

K: So, what'll you have, you girls?
A: I'll take a half pint of lager, please.
C: A glass of dry, red wine for me, please.
K: I suppose it's beer for the men? Ernst?
E: Yes please. Half a litre of bitter.

---

1 → *"I haven't lost face"*

At the pub

K: We call it a pint, Ernst, and if I might suggest it you should try a pint of real ale. It's darker than normal and is served at room temperature.
E: Why that? Too expensive to run a cooling system? Ha, ha.
J: No, that's not it, Ernst. It's because the yeast is still alive in the beer. I was drinking it last night[2] when I was preparing for school.
K: What were you doing last night Ernst while Jan was preparing his courses? Come on, tell the truth.
E: Well, last night I slept[3]. That's what I normally do in the night.
C: Hey, you know "last night" in English can mean "yesterday evening".
E: Of course I know that. I only joked[3] with you. I also know that you telephoned me. I walked[3] with my friend, Amy, when you phoned. We went to a small sea[4] in the near of[5] a village called Stone Road.
K: Excuse me, Ernst, could you fetch the beers?
E: No problem[6]. Barmaid, can you give me a tablet[7]? I have several beers.
B: A tablet? Well, I can give you one of my aspirins, if you like. Perhaps you should drink more slowly.
E: No, no, no! I talked[3] about something to carry the drinks on, made from[8] wood.
B: Oh, you mean a tray. Here you are.

(*Half an hour later, Ernst has the menu in his hand*).

E: We shall choose something from the card[9]. The barmaid looked[2] at me strangely[10] while I read[2] the card.
K: By the way, call her "miss" when you order. "Barmaid" is a bit unfriendly.

---

2 "Last night" means "gestern abend". → in der letzten Nacht = *during the last night*
3 → *last night I was sleeping*. This form stresses that the action was continuing, going on for a longer period. The dialogue contains several of these forms. → The correct forms are: *I was sleeping/ I was only joking/ I was walking/ I was talking about/ the barmaid was looking/ while I was reading*.
4 sea = Meer, die See → der See = *the lake*
5 Doesn't exist. → in der Nähe von = *near to* or *in the vicinity of*
6 It's a Germanism. In German the word "Problem" is used far too often. It creates a negative feeling. In English it is used far less. → *of course I will* or *okay, just a minute*
7 "Tablet" is a pill, like an aspirin. → Tablett = *tray*
8 → *made of* or *made out of*. Paper is made out of wood.
9 → *menu* = (Speise)karte. Menü = *dish of the day*
10 strangely = komisch → streng = *sternly*

At the pub

5

E: Well, she has taken a long time to take our order. Not good service.
A: Why Ernst, you have to go to the bar and order the food yourself. Didn't your friend, Amy, explain that? What were you doing together all yesterday evening?
E: Anna, do not be ordinary[11]! Or is it your Italian humour[12]? Hmm!

! Trouble-shoot that English

Wrong	Right
I worked when you phoned me. We drank Guinness while she ate.	I was working when you phoned. (This is possible, but if we want to stress that the action was going on for a longer period) We were drinking while she was eating.

Do you remember chapter 2? We looked at Present Simple and Continuous. Now we go to the Past Simple and Continuous. Do your best!

Verb Systems

Past Simple	Past Continuous
He phoned at 6 p.m. *They left after the party.*	*He was phoning at 6 p.m.* *They were leaving the party when I spoke to them.*
Action finished at a point in time, we know when.	Action was continuing through a period of time.

---

11 ordinary = normal, gewöhnlich → ordinär = *vulgar, primitive*
12 → *sense of humour*

At the pub

5

René: Ortrud, what were you really doing when I came into the office?
Ortrud: I was doing nothing that you would be interested in.

Strange but true!

Roses for the Lady

Like most other ladies, a resident of Canterbury called Killa, enjoys being presented with a lovely bunch of roses now and again. But unlike most English woman, Killa eats them. She also has a taste for expensive chocolates and is always happy with a bunch of celery. Just like your wife, you say. But no, Killa is a 300 pound female gorilla. A male boyfriend of hers also enjoys the odd gallon of beer.

Culture-crossing ▷ The English and their eating habits

Some "evil tongues" have said that English food is tasteless and expensive. Anyhow in the last ten years things have changed. The variety of food has improved and many exotic tastes from abroad have been integrated.

You can go to restaurants where you will probably pay more than in the many good pubs. In England you can find pubs almost around every corner, most of them also offer food. England is famous for its nice old pubs, some of which date back to the 14th century and earlier. That's atmosphere!

Just to give you a real-life taste of things we've got a small selection from the original menu from a pub near Hastings in Sussex. Notice what they include. For the price in DM, multiply by 2.8 (approximately).

At the pub

Starter

HOMEMADE CHICKEN LIVER PATE £3.95
SERVED WITH A SALAD GARNISH AND WARM TOAST

DEEPFRIED BREADED BRIE £3.50
WITH A CRANBERRY SAUCE. GARNISH & TOAST

NACHOS £2.50
COVERED IN SPICEY SALSA TOPPED WITH MELTED CHEESE

SPICEY CHICKEN WINGS £2.25
MARINATED AND BAKED IN A BARBEQUE SAUCE

SMOKED SALMON PATE £4.25
HOMEMADE SPICEY PATE WITH HOT TOAST

Main Course

LAMB CUTLETS WITH ROSMARY SAUCE £7.95
SERVED WITH NEW POTATOES AND FRESH SEASONAL VEGETABLES

ROASTED FRUITY BREAST OF DUCK £9.75
ROASTED DUCK SLICED AND WOK FINISHED WITH A HONEY AND ORANGE SAUCE
AND PRESENTED ON A BED OF FRESH FRUIT

SUPREME OF CHICKEN WITH GARLIC AND SAGE STUFFING £7.50
ACCOMPANIED BY A CAJUN TOMATO RELISH

POACHED DARNE OF SCOTTISH SALMON £8.75
SKINNED AND FILLETED FRESH SALMON, OVEN POACHED WITH LEMON JUICE,
BLACK PEPPER AND BUTTER AND DILL SAUCE

STUFFED TROUT £7.95
TROUT STUFFED WITH TARTAR AND BREADCRUMBS AND ACCOMPANIED BY A
SALAD GARNISH, NEW POTATOES AND FRESH VEGETABLES

Of course there are still those of the younger generation especially, who line up on Fridays to get their fish and chips. Excellent and tasty cod, plaice and haddock is drowned in fats and oils of the lowest quality. The fish is covered in a flour liquid and deep fried. Very fattening! You get mushy peas and soggy chips with it. People eat it out of newspaper! Totally unhealthy, but to some it's a way of life.

At the pub

 Now it's your turn

1. Help our Ernst!

Ernst is trying to order his evening meal at the bar in the Three Compasses, a thirteenth century pub near Canterbury.

Ernst: You, Miss, I die in front of hunger. I am waiting an eternity. Please give me a card.
Barmaid: I'm terribly sorry, sir. We're very busy at the moment.
Ernst: Good for your winnings, but I would like to willingly order. Today I tend to a fish.
Barmaid: This evening we have cod and chips, salmon and chips and plaice and chips.
Ernst: The fish hears it good on, but I want no chips. Better were potatoes.
Barmaid: But chips are potatoes cooked in boiling oil.
Ernst: Naturally, but I want no chips. Please, have you pommes frites?

2. Put the words in brackets into the correct form

a. The boss (address) a meeting of the firm's senior executives and sales staff. "Now, when my son (start) work here on Monday morning", he (say), "I want you to treat him just as you would treat all other new employee who (go) to take over the company in two year's time".

b. The boss (interview) a new secretary. "What sort of salary you (expect)? he asked.
"About 200 a week", (reply) the girl.
"£200", (say) the boss with a smile. "I (give) you that with pleasure. "With pleasure", she (say), "it (be) £500 a week."

3. Which is the best?

a. Canterbury is in the near of Dover.
Canterbury is near to Dover.
Canterbury is near of Dover.

At the pub

5

b. I was sitting on the London train when I was meeting Amy.
I sat on the London train when I met Amy.
I was sitting on the London train when I met Amy.

c. Translate into English:
1. Dieser Pub ist komplett aus Holz gebaut.
2. Gestern abend hatte ich Schweinekotelett mit Erbsen und Kartoffeln.
3. Kathy: Ernst, Sie wissen, daß es Ihre Runde ist. Sie müssen uns allen einen ausgeben.
   Ernst: Kein Problem. Die DM ist sehr stark.
   Kathy: Wenigstens war sie mal stark.

> **4. This is a very unfair exercise, but by looking at the names of the dishes can you guess what they cost?**

Match the price to the dish.

American Style Ribs	marinated in a spicy sauce served with rice and salad	£1.75
Chicken Burger	served with chips and salad	£8.50
Fish and Chips	local fish fried in batter with chips, peas	£5.25
Rump Steak	8 ozs	£4.95
Garlic Bread	a fresh baked baguette with garlic and herbs	£5.25
Cajun Chicken	served on a bed of salad	£395

By the way this menu comes from "The Horse shoe Inn", Herstmonceux, East Sussex.

At the pub

 Idiom after idiom!!!

German	Wrong	Right
Sich in den eigenen Finger schneiden.	Cut yourself in your own finger.	Score an own goal.
Einen Dickkopf haben.	Have a fat head.	Be pig-headed.
An die Decke gehen.	Go on the roof.	Hit the roof.

I'm lost

6

During his first weekend in the UK our hero, full of undertaking ghost[1] decides to prove[2] the landscape[3]. Ernst rents a car to make a trip to Cambridge. "It's a famous university city, just like Heidelberg. It's the sister town[4]", thought Ernst. As all the other students were busy he had to go alone. "It's good for me to stand on the own feet[5]", he said to himself.

After a close inspection of the circumstances leading to over a million car accidents around the world, investigators have proved conclusively that the part of a car most likely to cause an accident is the nut behind the wheel.

➔ Ernst at the car rental company "Rent-a-wreck" in Canterbury

C = Clerk; E = Ernst; P = Policeman

C: So we've got a very nice little Gonda Civilian here, not too aggressive on petrol. It might suit you.

E: Oh, at home in Heidelberg I drive a BMW three, so I think I will be consequent[6] here in England also[7]. Do you rent[8] BMWs?

C: Well, yes we do have BMWs for hire. I thought you might prefer a more economical model.

---

1 ➔ Unternehmensgeist = *spirit of enterprise*, here: *with a spirit of adventure*
2 prove = beweisen ➔ prüfen = *check* or *test*, here: *to take a look at*
3 landscape = Landschaft ➔ *scenery* or *countryside*
4 ➔ *twin town. Heidelberg is twinned with Cambridge*
5 ➔ *to stand on my own feet*. "Own" always takes a possessive, "my, your, his, her, our, their." *She has her own car. I want to buy my own house.*
6 consequent = folglich ➔ konsequent = *consistent*, here: *I'll do it, too*
7 There are two words for "auch" ➔ *also* and *too*. We use them in different ways. We normally put "also" before the main verb. *Her car also runs on diesel.* "too" goes to the end of the phrases or sentence. *The pound is a strong currency, too*
8 rent or hire = mieten ➔ vermieten = *rent out* or *hire out*

I'm lost

E: No, money plays no role⁹. I drive¹⁰ a BMW since five years. What's the cost?
C: It's £80 per day, mileage is included.
E: That's expensive. At home I can have it 50 percent cheaper.
C: I'm sure you can. But here we have a thousand tourists everyday with all the costs that tourists create.
E: Okay. I'll need a left-hand drive.
C: Oh dear. We don't have continental cars. You'll get used to right-hand drive very quickly.
E: Well, I guess I can't alter it¹¹. I'll take the BMW3.

(*Ernst in Cambridge. He drives past the magnificent university buildings, down a side street.*)

E: (*to himself*) No I wanted to get to the north end. And...
P: (*knocking on Ernst's window*) Excuse me, sir, you can't park here by the river. These are double yellow lines. No parking under any circumstances.
E: I'm not parking. I've lost myself¹².
P: We've all got personal problems of one sort or another. Now, pull yourself together and drive your car to an official parking area, or I'll be forced to book you.
E: Hmm, slowly this town is becoming unsympathetic¹³ to me. I am driving¹⁰ around here since one hour¹⁰. You could spare time¹⁴ by showing me the way.
P: Alright. Alright. Just to make sure you don't cause any accidents I'll guide you to where you want to go.
E: Thank you, Mr policeman¹⁵, that's what I call engagement¹⁶.
P: Could you just follow my car, sir?
E: It is a pleasure to me¹⁷.

---

9 The idiom in English → *money is no object*
10 → *I have driven a BMW for 5 years.* Present Perfect plus for/since (seit) *I have driven/been driving around for one hour.*
11 → *I have no choice* or *I can't do anything about it*
12 → *I've got lost* or *I am lost*
13 be sympathetic = Mitgefühl haben → sympathisch = *nice*, unsympathisch = *unfriendly* or *unpleasant*
14 spare = Ersatz → Zeitsparen = *save time*
15 → You should address a policeman with "*constable*"
16 English "engagement" = Verlobung → German "Engagement" = *motivation*, here: *commitment*
17 → *It'll be a pleasure*

I'm lost

6 ⚠ Trouble-shoot that English

Wrong	Right
I'm driving since two hours.	I have been driving for two hours.
We work on this project since December.	We have worked on this project since December.

It's a nightmare for Germans to decide between "for" and "since" and what tense to use with them. Let's get it sorted out once and for all!

(TIP)

Contrast between "for" and "since"

FOR	SINCE
we use it when we are talking about a period of time	... when we talk about a point in time like a date
for six months	*since last October*
for twenty years	*since 1995*
for a long time	*since yesterday*

DANGER!

When we use for/since, we must take the Present Perfect or the Present Perfect Continuous (forms built with "have").

I have lived in Heidelberg for ten years
or
I have been living in Heidelberg for ten years
(Ich wohne seit zehn Jahren in Heidelberg)

We have expected trouble since the beginning of the year
or
We have been expecting trouble since the beginning of the year
(Seit Anfang des Jahres rechnen wir mit Ärger)

I'm lost

6

> As a rule of thumb!

SENTENCES WITH FOR OR SINCE NEED "HAVE"

On holiday

Conchita: I have become very religious since I came on this holiday.
René: Good heavens Conchita, why is that?
Conchita: Because I didn't believe in hell until we got here.

Robert: The weather has been terrible for the whole two weeks.
René: That can't be. Why are you so brown?
Robert: I didn't get brown from the sun. That's rust caused by the rain.

Culture-crossing ▷ The media in England

What else is going on in England? People can't be drinking beer all the time, can they? As a nation the little "Englanders" read a lot. There are many bookshops and books are relatively cheap. They have a good selection and most things have been translated into English.

The bookshop

Visiting a bookshop in England is more than just buying books. Firstly the selection is huge. You can browse through books for hours. When you've selected a few, you can drift off to the special café which many of the bookshops have at their disposal. There you drink and dream books.

Newspapers

We have the "heavies". These are newspapers containing lots of information such as The Times, The Independent, The Financial Times, Telegraph and the Sundays. They're not as heavy going as Die Zeit, but they take some time to read. Every country has its tabloid press and the

I'm lost

"island" does, too. If you want scandal, sex and sport browse through the Sun, Mirror, Star, Mail. There is also a multitude of regional and specialist newspapers.

TV

For those of us who can't read we have the TV. In addition to the five main channels, many people have satellite or digital TV, which brings them another forty or fifty stations. If you're not careful you could get brainwashed.

Radio

Radio broadcasts in England differ a lot from German ones. English radio is very interactive. You have a lot of "phone-in" shows, and unfortunately a hell of a lot of advertising. You do get a lot of competitions with prizes which can't be turned down.

In England the public radio stations are numbered 1 – 4. Then there are the many private stations, such as Capital FM in London. Being young and dynamic, we'd like to recommend the Midlands and Trent FM (96.2). That'll shock you enough. Their motto is "less talk, more music".

Now it's your turn

1. Help our Ernst!

Ernst on a weekend trip to Cambridge. (**E** = Ernst; **G** = Gentlemen)

E: Excuse, sir. I'm ferseaching to find a food local namely The Blue Boar. Know you where it befinds itself?

G: Oh, let me see. You drive along this road, turn right at the end. Then you follow the road over the river. It's first left after the bridge.

E: If I remember me well, this road along, right at the end, on top of the bridge, first left.

G: Yes, that's about right. Are you sure you'll remember?

E: Thank you the afterquestion, no problem. I make me on the socks. Cheers.

I'm lost

2. Put the verbs in brackets in the correct form

Anna: Jim and I (be) together for six months, but I (give) him up.
Conchita: Why? What (be) wrong with him? He always (look) handsome, well-dressed. He (have) a lot of money. And you (seem) to like him a lot.
Anna: He really (get) on my nerves since last Christmas. He (have) a number of bad habits.
Conchita: We all (have) those.
Anna: One of them was that he always (stir) his tea or coffee – even in restaurants – with his left hand.
Conchita: What (be) wrong with that?
Anna: Everyone else uses a spoon.

3. Which is the best?

a. I'll buy a bottle of champagne. Money plays no role.
   I'll buy a bottle of champagne. Money is no object.
   I'll buy a bottle of champagne. Money plays no part.

b. Ernst hasn't arrived back from Cambridge.
   Perhaps he's got lost.
   Perhaps he's lost himself.
   Perhaps he has himself lost.

c. Anna wants to try to spare some money.
   Anna wants to try to save some money.
   Anna wants to try to save some spare money.

4. Translate into English

a. Conchita ist niemals Auto gefahren.
b. Anna fährt seit vier Jahren Auto.
c. Ernst ist tatsächlich ein sehr sympathischer Mensch.
d. Die neue Regierung ist seit 1998 im Amt.

I'm lost

Time for an idiom

German	Wrong	Right
Er ist nicht auf den Kopf gefallen.	He didn't fall on his head.	He's no fool.
Er hat sich sämtliche Beine ausgerissen.	He's pulled out all his legs.	He bent over backwards.
Hart am Ball bleiben.	Stay hard on the ball.	Stick to it.

A game called cricket

7

Our hero and his course colleagues are invited along to Kent Cricket Ground to watch a match on Wednesday evening. Two of their teachers, Roy from Australia and Ian from Scotland accompany them. After watching the game for two hours it is time for some sandwiches and beer in the clubhouse. Not every foreign person understands cricket.

"I've learnt some white man's magic," said the African chief when he returned to his country after a short stay in England.
"Tell me about it," asked his brother.
"First, you must make a smooth piece of ground and get grass to grow on it. Then you carefully tend the grass. After that you place some sticks in the grass. Some men dress themselves in all-white clothes. Two of the men carry pieces of wood called 'bats' and another man has to throw a red ball. After some running about between the sticks by two of the men and some throwing of the red ball, it will begin to rain."

In the clubhouse

E = Ernst; P = Pyotr; R = Roy; I = Ian; A = Anna; C = Conchita; J = Jan

E: Listen people, I go[1] and fetch a tray with all the drinks and the sandwiches.
P: Good idea, Ernst. You're certainly the best organiser here.
R: "The best organiser", Pyotr. Don't forget your definite articles.
P: Thank you, but they are your definite articles and not mine.
C: Talking of useless things what on earth do you English see in that game of cricket? I don't understand the point of it.
I: Well, first of all neither Roy nor myself are English. And as a Scotsman I quite agree with you. The game makes no sense.

---

1 *I'll go, you'll give, I'll fetch, I'll be back, you'll have*. See our trouble-shoot corner for more details.

A game called cricket

R: We Australians borrowed the game from the Brits and we've shown them how to play it ever since.

E: Hi, everyone. I've got the goodies. Hey, Roy, that cricket game[2] was barbaric[3]. What was happening out there? I know you give[1] us a lecture on that.

R: Well, I will give you some information about it if that's what you want.

A: We certainly do! And I like your accent so much.

P: I see your Italian blood is boiling, but try to keep yourself under control.

R: Well, you have two teams all dressed in white. One is the batting team, they sit off the field and wait for their turn. The other one is the bowling team. They stand around on the field. One of them bowls or throws the red ball at the wickets. The wickets are the three pieces of wood ... (*fade out*).

E: (*fade in*) ...Well, thank you for that, Roy, but I think it was pearls before the pigs[4]. I must have overheard[5] a lot because ...

C: ... you didn't understand anything.

E: Hit it in the black[6]. I fetch[1] some more beers and perhaps we can talk about other sports. In Germany we like sport.

P: You like to win. I don't know if you like to play sport.

E: It's the same. I'm back[1] in a moment.

(*Three minutes later*)

A: What sports do you play in Australia, Roy?

R: Well, we go in for cricket, rugby, Australian football which is a rougher form of rugby. Nothing for you Europeans. We also play a lot of squash and of course there's the whole range of water sports.

E: It seems to me these are all arts[7] of sports from England.

I: From Britain, you mean. You may be right.

---

2 → *match* – football match, tennis match, cricket match, but round or game of golf
3 → *fantastic*; in English "barbaric" means "having the characteristics of a barbarian" = scheußlich
4 The correct idiom in English is → *cast pearls to the swine* here: *it was casting ...*
5 overhear = zufällig lauschen → verpassen = *miss*
6 → ins Schwarze treffen = *hit the bullseye*
7 art = Kunst → Arten von = *types* or *kinds*

A game called cricket

E: Yes, and how is it with[8] the Scots? You have[1] your own parliament soon. What typical things do you have in Scotland?
I: Well, the first thing I should say is that most sports were invented in Britain. And the Scots have done their bit, too.
E: No, you are misinformed[9]. We Germans win most competitions. It's a statistical fact.
I: I said "we invented" most of the games.
E: Name me examples[10]!
I: Football, cricket, squash, badminton, golf, rugby. And in Scotland we've got our Highland games.
J: It looks like you've been caught with your trousers down, Ernst.
E: Hmm, it appears I stand alone[11] in this round[12].
C: Not at all, Ernst, Jan is only pulling your leg.
E: Pulling my legs, with trousers down. I understand the world no more[13].

❗ Trouble-shoot that English

Wrong	Right
I come to your place at 10 o'clock.	I'll come to your place at 10 o'clock.
Anna buys an ice-cream after the course has finished.	Anna will buy an ice-cream after the course has finished.

We have to be careful when we want to talk about the future. Unlike in German very often we need to put "will" (werden), or when speaking "'ll", into the sentence.

---

8 → *what about the Scots?*
9 "You are misinformed" is very abrupt. Your conservation partner will lose face. It's better to take another alternative → *"You've got the wrong end of the stick"* or *"I can't quite share your opinion"*
10 → *can you give me a few examples?* or *let's hear a few then*
11 → *I'm in the minority* or *I'm on my own in my opinion*
12 → *this group*. A "round" is used to speak about "a round of golf" or "a round of beer".
13 English idiom → *I don't know whether I'm coming or going* or *I don't know what's going on any more*

A game called cricket

7

> **TIP**
>
> We build the Simple Future with "will" or "'ll" + Infinitive
>
> *Ernst will pay for the cinema this evening.*
> (Ernst zahlt für das Kino heute abend.)
>
> *We'll see each other tomorrow then.*
> (Wir sehen uns dann morgen.)
>
> *I'll pick you up in two hours.*
> (Ich hol dich in zwei Stunden ab.)
>
> There are several other ways to talk about the future:
>
> Definite action in future:
> *Conchita is teaching at the evening school tomorrow.*
>
> When we intend to do something in the future:
> *I'm going to run a marathon next year.*
> (Ich habe vor, nächstes Jahr einen Marathon zu laufen.)

"We are going to send a rocket to Pluto," announced the Americans proudly. "It'll have six men on board and will stay on Pluto for six weeks before it comes back to Earth."
"That's nothing", bragged the Russians. "Next week we're launching our spaceship with 300 men and women to start the first colony on Uranus."
"We Scots are better than both of you", said Ian, the Scottish scientist. "We're going to send a rocket straight to the sun."
"Don't be stupid! It'll melt before it gets there", was the reply.
"Of course it won't," shouted Ian. "We're sending it up at night."

A game called cricket

⊞ Culture-crossing ▷ The English and their sport

Leisure time and what do the active Brits do? They have a lot of types of "sports" which they mostly perform "just for fun". We have the more physical types who meet on Saturday mornings or afternoons. The footballers (22 of them) kick a round piece of leather around a football pitch. Rougher fellows also play their game, rugby, with a ball. Unfortunately someone sat on the ball so it's become oblong and difficult to kick. Perhaps for this reason they tend to pick it up and run with it. They also tend to sing rude songs together after the game while drinking their beer.

Sunday morning is more for the cricketers. We've talked enough about them. Of course, after sweaty sports the little "Englander" has to rush into the pub, the centre of cultural life. He has to rush because the barman might call "last orders, please" at 10.30pm or 11 o'clock. And there many a lad will play the beloved game of darts. The players stand six or seven feet away from a circle of cork divided into triangles, each with its own number of points. They throw little spears with feathers at the end into the cork circle. "501" is a famous game of this type. You start with 501 points and try to get zero as quickly as possible. And it's vitally important to drink beer and eat crisps in between your shots. More intellectual islanders sit around tables in pubs and take part in the "pub quiz". It is a "beery" form of Trivial Pursuit.

More skilful than the above-mentioned activities are squash and badminton. Fitter English men and women go to the courts after work. In the case of squash two people hammer a harmless rubber ball at a wall and sweat a lot. The badminton specialist clouts a bunch of feathers over a net. And afterwards that wonderful pint of beer. Whatever sport you do, you have to replace your lost liquids! Fishing and golf are very popular and inexpensive, too.

According to a new survey, 76 percent of men would rather watch a football game than have sex. My question is, why do we have to choose? Why do you think they invented half-time?

A game called cricket

7

Good sport

The trouble with being a good sport is
that you have to lose to prove it.

Golf for Ghouls

Usch: Robert, you promised you'd be home at 4.00. It's now 8.00.
Rob: Sweetheart, just listen to me. Pour old René is dead. He just fell down on the eighth green.
Usch: Oh, that's awful.
Rob: It certainly was. For the rest of the game it was hit the ball, drag René, hit the ball, drag René.

 Now it's your turn!

1. Help our Ernst!

Ernst has just found out he can play golf in Canterbury for just a few pounds. Astonished he runs to the telephone. He has been told to phone Canterbury Golf Club:

E = Ernst; **R** = Receptionist

E: Hallo, I am the Ernst Lachnit. I have become a news that I can play a round for £9.
R: That's right, sir. £5 for nine holes, £9 for eighteen. When would you like to play?
E: Today we have Monday. I had played overtomorrow, yes midweek.
R: Okay, so if I've got it, you want to play in the middle of the week. What about Wednesday?
E: Wednesday, exactly. I have you already said. We are to two.
R: I beg your pardon. You're to what?
E: No, not two what! Two players. What other?
R: Just a moment, sir.
E: (*to himself*) That was a hard piece of work.

A game called cricket

2. Put the verbs in brackets in the correct form

"Roll up, roll up! (Buy) this miraculous cure for old age and colds. Even rigor mortis can be cured! Roll up, roll up!" (call) the fair ground doctor. He soon (collect) a large crowd.
"This mixture (cure) old age. Just (look) at me to see the proof of its power. I (be) over two hundred and fifty years old."
One astonished man in the crowd (turn) to his beautiful assistant and asked, "is he really over two hundred years old?"
"I'm afraid I can't really say," she said, "but next year I will have been working with him for 95 years."

3. Which is the best?

a. What is the tastiest kind of English beer?
   What is the tastiest art of English beer?
   What is the tastiest English beer type?

b. I'm sorry, it was very loud in the underground.
   I missed a lot.
   I missed a lot of what you were saying.
   I overheard what you were saying.

c. That's very interesting! But how is it with taxes?
   That's very interesting! But what is it with taxes?
   That's very interesting! But what about taxes?

4. Translate a few simple sentences into English

a. Ernst: Hi, Conchita, ich komme dich morgen besuchen.
   Vielleicht können wir zusammen schwimmen gehen.

b. Ich glaube, ich stehe allein da mit meiner Meinung.

c. Das ist genau richtig. Sie haben ins Schwarze getroffen.

A game called cricket

7 Here an idiom, there an idiom, everywhere an ...

German	Wrong	Right
Die Kirche im Dorf lassen.	Leave the church in the village.	Don't exaggerate.
Er kann ihr nicht das Wasser reichen.	He can't reach her the water.	He can't hold a candle to her.
Von allen guten Geistern verlassen.	Left by all the good ghosts.	To have taken leave of one's senses.

An English rose

Well, it happens to the best of us. Ernst Lachnit has lost his heart, not in Heidelberg, but in England. He was out one evening at the theatre when he met Jenny, a nurse from the local hospital. She was so friendly and open with a smile in her eyes and a great little figure. Ernst fell head over heels in love. And wonders never cease, Jenny was interested in Ernst, too. And, of course, it was all very good for his English. (Not that that really mattered). Jenny and Ernst go to London for a get-a-way weekend.

Mike and Alison decided to start living together. One Saturday evening Alison came home very late. She tried to creep quietly into bed without waking Mike but he is a very light sleeper. He switched on the bedside light and watched her undress.
"Where the devil is your underwear?", he thundered.
"My God!" cried Alison in anguish. "I've been robbed."

The happy young couple are at the musical, Evita. It is the interval.

J = Jenny; E = Ernst

J: That was a great performance. What did you think?

E: Yes, the actual[1] show was excellent. Do you often go out to see a musical or a theatre piece[2]?

J: Very rarely. As a nurse I don't have much time. It's difficult to fit anything in.

E: Ah yes. Your profession[3]. I've heard that the salary isn't very good. But I think if you would work[4] more hours you would earn more money.

---

1 actual = tatsächlich → aktuell = *current* or *present* here: *today's show* ...
2 → Theaterstück = *play*
3 profession = Beruf. But "profession" often refers to a specific number of job-types = lawyers, doctors, teachers etc. → In the dialogue "*your job*" would be better.

An English rose

8

J: Yes, but there's a limit to the number of hours a person can work in a week.

E: But you will certainly get a rent[5] at the end of your working life.

J: I don't quite know what you mean. I'm actually paying for a mortgage at the bank at the moment. I'm buying my own house. I'm an owner occupier.

E: No, I was talking about when you are pensioned[6].

J: Oh, you're asking if I'll get a pension. Yes, I will. I hope so.

E: If you would want[4] to change your job, would you take your pension with you in full?

J: I certainly would.

E: Hey, look, it's time for the third act. Let's go back in.

(*Several hours later at an Indian restaurant*)

E: My God! If I would have known[4] how spicy that meal was going to be, I would never have taken[7] it.

J: Yes, Madras curry is quite hot if you're not used to it. Never mind. Let's take the opportunity and walk home in the fresh evening air. Waiter!

(*Half an hour later*)

E: Oh dear! It's further than I thought to the pension[8].

J: More years to work for it, you mean.

E: No, more kilometres.

J: Oh, to the boarding house. We call them boarding houses or bed & breakfast.

E: What a pity it's so late. If the shops would be[4] open, we could buy a bottle of champagne and really celebrate. So a beautiful evening[9].

J: That's no problem. All the wine shops and off-licences are open until midnight.

....

4 Conditional sentences. It is a typical mistake to put "will" or "would" in the dependent clause. → It should read: *"If you worked more hours you would earn more money", "If you wanted to change your job, would you take ...", "If I had known how spicy that meal was ...", "If shops were open ...", "If you buy alcohol ..."*

5 rent = Miete → Rente = *pension*

6 → *when you have retired*

7 Not "take a meal" but → *"order a meal"*. *"I would never have ordered ..."*

8 pension = Rente → Pension = *boarding house* or *B&B*

9 → *what a beautiful evening!*

An English rose

E: You make jokes[10]! When do the staff sleep?

J: Oh, people work shifts, or students do it for a bit of extra income. Many shops work all the weekend, too. And sometimes small shops simply stay open to make more turnover. And the members of the public are given a better service. Isn't it the same in Germany?

E: Most of our shops close at six o'clock in the evening. And Saturday afternoons and Sundays. But if you will buy[4] alcohol and champagne, you can get it at any petrol station.

J: Alcohol at a petrol station? That's absolutely not permitted here. We're trying to take drink off the road. Do you know most of my accident patients come...

❗ Trouble-shoot that English

Wrong	Right
If you would work harder, I would pay you more.	If you worked harder, I would pay you more.
If she would want to change her job, she'd have problems.	If she wanted to change her job, she'd have problems.

"If"-sentences are not really as bad as they seem. Here's a short overview of the form. Watch where you put your "wills" and "woulds".

> **TIP**
>
> **Conditional sentences**
>
> Future:
> *If I see you tomorrow, I'll give you her telephone number.*
> **If + Present**   **will + Grundform**
> Wenn ich dich morgen sehe, gebe ich dir ihre Telefonnummer.

---

10 The idiom is → *you must be joking*

An English rose

8

Possibility:
If you lent me your car, I would be very careful with it.
If + Past   would + Grundform
Wenn du mir dein Auto leihen würdest, wäre ich sehr vorsichtig damit.

Condition in the past (the "already too late" form):
If I had known, I would never have employed you.
If + Past Perfect   would + have + partizip
Wenn ich das gewußt hätte, hätte ich Sie nie eingestellt.

Jenny: That's too quick, Ernst.
Ernst: But I believe in love at first sight. It saves such a lot of time.

Jenny: I don't know if you're a reliable man.
Ernst: Of course, I am. I'm always there.
Jenny: Well, let's just say that whenever you want me, there you are.

Ernst: So how about it?
Jenny: Your place or mine?
Ernst: If it's going to be a hassle, forget it!

If capitalism depended on the intellectual quality of the Conservative party, it would end about lunchtime tomorrow.

Culture-crossing ▷ Leisure time and the opposite sex

So what about the birds and the bees on the island? Well, sometimes several young men and women form a group of six or eight people and pursue a pastime together. They might go walking in the hills, enduring rain and storms to reach their goal. And afterwards, somewhere in the hills, the warm and cosy pub with a pint of real ale. Then there's the eternal football or rugby match. Some young women join their men

An English rose

and go to a match, stand around in the cold, freeze and shout when their team scores. That's love, isn't it?

Just like in the old days there's the cinema. There's a wide range of films in Britain and film-going is still "in". Sitting holding hands with your loved one and crunching popcorn or sucking ice-cream. What more do you want?

Still, most couples have their own favourite pubs where they feel at home. The girls drink juices spiked with vodka or an equally dangerous short, and the boys have their lagers, real ales and the bitters. Nowadays it's "cool" to drink Mexican beer "on the neck" (out of the bottle).

After all this drinking we get hungry. It's already eleven in the evening, so it's time for a Chinese or Indian take-away curry. And off to his or her flat or house to watch the goggle-box!

Young English men and women do have some strange behaviour patterns. They tend to go out with each other ("go out" is a synonym for sleeping together), and then to get "engaged" (verlobt) which is a warning sign that this person belongs to me. Some people often get engaged several times.

Rob: Why do all the men find Anna so attractive?
René: Because of her speech problem.
Rob: Her speech problem?
René: Yes. She can't say "no".

Anna: I'll pour the drinks. What will you have – gin and platonic?
Ernst: I was hoping for whisky and sofa.

An English rose

Now it's your turn

1. Help our Ernst!

Ernst: Two cards for the seance at seventeen o'clock, please.
Ticket clerk: Sorry, I've not quite got it. What do you want?
Ernst: Are you heavy in hearing? For Total Recall, two cards.
Ticket clerk: Right, two tickets for Total Recall.
Ernst: Exactly. And still something. I need a little something sweet. Man grants himself otherwise nothing.
Ticket clerk: So, you'd like some chocolate or something like that?
Ernst: Haven't I said that? You are a sleeping cap.

2. Put in the missing verbs

a. Exercise is nonsense:
If you (be) healthy, you don't need it;
if you (be) sick, you shouldn't take it.

b. Waddling around like a recently impregnated hippopotamus ...
Paul Gasgoigne had become a bona fide wobble-bottom ...
But if football (be) to fail him, he could choose another career, for example, as Father Christmas, a barrage balloon ...

3. Which is correct?

a. My flat is too expensive.
I pay DM 600 for my pension every month.
I pay DM 600 for my rent every month.
I pay DM 600 for my board every month.

b. If God would have wanted man to fly, he would have created him with wings.
If God had wanted man to fly, he would have created him with wings.
If God had wanted man to fly, he had created him with wings.

An English rose

An idiom a day keeps the doctor away

German	Wrong	Right
Funk mal nicht dazwischen.	Don't spark in between.	Please, don't interrupt.
Wo brennt's?	Where's it burning?	What's up? What's wrong?
Das ist für den Arsch.	That's for the arse.	That's a washout.
Sich Hals über Kopf verlieben.	Fall neck over head in love.	Fall head over heels in love.

Going shopping

9

Ernst, Conchita and Pyotr go to London at the weekend. They want to do some shopping at the famous stores, Harrods and Selfridges. Pyotr especially wants to visit Portobello Road to see if he can get any bargains. He's not so interested in shopping in the big, expensive shops. Ernst hopes to find a Burberry jacket at a cheap price. Conchita prefers just to look. She's fascinated by the large selection.

In a shop

Customer: "Do you take anything off for cash?"
Sales Assistant: "Sir, this is a shop, not a striptease joint."

It's a nightmare travelling in London these days.
The other day I had to stand all the way from
Marble Arch to Hammersmith
– and I was in a taxi.

At Harrods

C = Conchita; **P** = Pyotr; **E** = Ernst; **A** = Assistant; **S** = Salesman

C: Jesus Christ, I've never seen so many different types of food in one place.
P: Or in all places put together. Back in Russia we don't have these types of shops.
E: You don't have much to put in them, what[1]?
P: That's not quite true. We have some products nowadays, but normal people can't afford to buy them.

---

1 → *do you?* For "nä", "wohl", "wa", "gell", "was" we use question tags: "do you?", "doesn't he?", "have they?", "won't they?" etc. In this dialogue: *do you, aren't they, are they?*

Going shopping

C: My goodness! Look at these pheasants hanging upside down dead over the counter. Kilometers[2] of them.
E: My dear Conchita, you don't have them hanging live in Portugal, or[1]?
C: Ha, Ha! I don't think we have them at all.
E: I think these birds are rather expensive compared with ours in Germany, nä[1]? And look, the quality is not good. They're not fresh, as you can see, or[1]?
P: I read in a Sherlock Holmes novel that the birds must hang and rot with the shot still in them, like a good brie cheese.
E: I see. And the English shoot their brie cheeses and let them rot, too, do they? We can control[3] your information. I'll go to the shop assistant.
C: Come on, Ernst. Leave it! Let's go up to the jackets.
E: Okay. Exceptionally[4]. Normally I finish what I begin, but I'm also interested in a Burberry jacket.
C: Oh, Ernst, I can't imagine what Jenny sees in you. Come on.

(*In the jacket department*)
E: Excuse me, sir, these are not the prices for the Burberry jackets, or[1]?
A: They are indeed, sir, and cheap at the price.
E: Cheap? I think these prices are over the clouds[5].
A: Would you care to try on this fine jacket? It's a slightly different style and a little more inexpensive.
E: Okay. Moment[6]. There. Oh goodness! It's much too small[7].
A: Too small? Let's try a size bigger, shall we?
E: No, no! I mean it's too narrow around my middle. I think I'd better forget about it. Thank you. Good bye.

(*An hour later, in Portobello Road*)
S: (*at a stall*) Here's a lovely Burberry jacket, just your size, governor, and just at the right price.

---

2 → *miles of them*
3 control = kontrollieren → überprüfen = *check*
4 exceptionally = außergewöhnlich → ausnahmsweise = *just this time* or *as an exception*
5 → schwindelerregend hoch = *sky high*
6 → *just a minute/moment!*
7 → eng (bei Kleidern) = *tight*

Going shopping

9

E: Yes, it lies very well[8]. (*to Pyotr*) It only cost half of the one at Harrods. Right, sir, I'll take it.

(*Next day, after Anna had noticed a hole in the jacket, Ernst is back at the stall.*)

A different salesman: What can I do for you, sir?
E: Please look at this hole. This is one of your jackets!
S: That may well be, but we aren't taking anything back. No guarantees here.
E: But that is impossible[9].
S: It's very possible, mate. You could have done that yourself. See, you got it at a knockdown price.
P: Come on, Ernst! You've had bad luck, that's all.
E: That may not be possible[10]! Where's the English sense of fair play?

[!] Trouble-shoot that English

Wrong	Right
You have enough money with you, or?	You have enough money with you, don't you?
We'll be having our meeting next week, or not?	We'll be having our meeting next week, won't we?

(TIP 1)

Question Tags are only short phrases and they are easily forgotten. In German they exist in the form "nicht wahr", as a sort of universal phrase. There are several regional forms like "woll", "gell", "nä", "wat", etc. In English we have a more complicated form.

---

8 → *it fits very well* = es paßt/sitzt gut
9 This phrase makes no sense in English. → *But that's unfair* or *You can't do that*
10 → *this simply can't be true!*

Going shopping

*This beer **is** expensive, **isn't** it?* = *Dieses Bier ist teuer, oder?*

*Your joke **wasn't** (-) very funny, **was** (+) it?*

*Ernst **played** (+) golf yesterday, **didn't** (-) he?*

*You **know** the price, **don't** you?*

*We **can** afford to go to dinner, **can't** we?*

*They **mustn't** (-) drive without a license, **must** (+) they?*

If the main sentence is positive, the Question Tag is negative.
If the main sentence is negative, the Question Tag is positive.
The verb in the Question Tag is built up from the verb in the main sentence.

(TIP 2)

When we say "I am" in the main sentence, we say "aren't I?" in the Tag.

*I'**m** always the last to know, **aren't** I?*

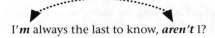

At the store

Ernst: I can try on that dress in the window, can't I?
Shop assistant: Well, I'd prefer it if you used the changing room.

Going shopping

9

Ernst: Money isn't everything.
Jenny: Ernst, whoever told you that?
Ernst: My boss.

Culture-crossing ▷ Shopping in Britain

In Britain most shops are open from 9am to 6pm. In the big towns stores are also open on Sundays. Supermarkets and food shops stay open until ten o'clock in the evening, so there is no stress.

You can buy clothes rather cheaply in Britain (not in the centre of London, of course). Getting the size right is a problem. Here's a table to help you.

Shoes	UK	4	5	6	7	8	9	10
	Europe	37	38	39	41	42	43	44
Men's shirts	UK		15		$15^{1/2}$ 16		$16^{1/2}$	17
	Europe		38		39 41		42	43
Men's suits	UK		38		40	42		44
	Europe		48		50	52		54
Blouses and dresses	UK		10		12	14		16
	Europe		38		40	42		44

But when you choose something, please do not put it into your bag before you have been to the till (cash desk) to pay for it. It may be presumed that you are trying to steal it.

The unpleasant part is paying for something. The currency in England is the pound sterling. We have 1p, 2p, 5p, 20p, 50p and £1 coins. The notes are £5, £10, £20 and £50. In Scotland they issue their own notes. They can also be used in Britain.

If you find yourself without food and drink in the evening, search out the nearest "off-licence". These places are open late, normally managed by Pakistanis or Indians, because some modern English people are too lazy to work in the evenings. You can buy beer and wine, bread, vegetables and anything you want. Most of them even have a large selection of videos nowadays.

Going shopping

9

Tailor: Your suit will be ready in six weeks, sir.
Customer: Six weeks! But God made the whole world in only six days!
Tailor: Quite true, sir. But look what state the world is in.

Ernst went into a bakery.
Ernst: How much for these two pies?
The girl behind the counter said "90 pence".
Ernst: How much is it for one?
Girl: Sixty pence.
Ernst: I'll have the other one.

Now it's your turn

1. Help our Ernst!

Ernst: Sir, I have seen a trouser in the show-window. I had proved it on.
Assistant: I beg your pardon? Oh, you want to try on this pair of trousers? I'll just get your size. What is your size by the way? Forty-one, forty-two?
Ernst: I do not now my greatness in England. Have you a measurement?
Assistant: Yes, I'll just take your measurements to be certain. Yes, 44. Good.
Ernst: Have you a room where I can pull me round?
Assistant: Yes, behind the curtain.

2. Put the words in the brackets into the correct form

Ernst at the border returning from a holiday in France. He is trying to get into an Arab country. The poor fellow is stopped at the border.
"This bottle has something in it, (nicht wahr)?" asked the customs officer, taking a large bottle from Ernst's suitcase.
"Oh", said Ernst. "You can see it's Holy Water from Lourdes, (nicht wahr)?"

Going shopping

"Hmmm!" muttered the customs officer as he took the top off the bottle and sniffed the liquid inside. Then he tasted some of it. "It looks, smells and tastes very much like whisky to me, sir, (nicht wahr)?"
"Good Heavens!" replied Ernst, "It's another miracle, (nicht wahr)?".

3. Put in the correct question tag (nicht wahr) form

a. Ernst always seems to make the same mistakes, ...
b. You'll give me back the money you owe me, ...
c. The reader ought to get this one wrong, ...
d. But he shouldn't take it all too seriously, ...
e. I'm tired of all these question tags, ...
f. Conchita misunderstood what Ernst wanted to say, ...

4. How good are you at buying in Britain?

1. a bottle of
2. half a dozen
3. a tube of
4. a block of
5. a pint of
6. a box of
7. 1/2 pound of
8. a packet of
9. a bar of
10. a bunch of

a. soap
b. chocolate
c. milk
d. Nivea sun tan oil
e. matches
f. rolls
g. razorblades
h. roses
i. butter
j. toothpaste

Going shopping

 Idioms for idiots!

German	Wrong	Right
Wollen Sie mich anmachen?	Want you to make me on?	Are you trying to chat me up?
Sich durchwursteln.	To sausage through.	To muddle through.
Du hast einen Dachschaden.	You've got roof damage.	You've got a screw loose.

An apple a day keeps the doctor away

10

Well, it can happen to the best of us. Ernst started to get sick. He must have eaten something not very fresh. Anyhow, he got really bad stomach ache. Jenny wasn't around so he had to go to a doctor's by himself. It's not so easy to describe your aches and pains in a foreign language. It's all a source of misunderstandings.

Ernst was waiting in a doctor's reception when a young girl came out of the surgery sobbing bitterly.
Ernst: What's the matter?
Girl: The doctor's just told me I'm pregnant.
Ernst went in for his turn.
Ernst: Is that young lady really pregnant?
Doc: No, but telling her cured her hiccups.

Aches and pains

E = Ernst; **R** = Receptionist; **D** = Dr Disney; **C** = Conchita

R: Can I help you, sir?
E: I hope you can. I telephoned with[1] you two hours ago. I've eaten something that didn't agree with me. I have bad stomach pains.
R: Okay. The doctor can see you in an hour.
E: Oh, but I have my private medical insurance. Look! I would like that[2] the doctor sees me as soon as possible.
R: Well, your card is very elegant, but here everybody has to wait in the queue.
E: Do you mean I have to wait the same like[3] the people with normal medical insurance?

---

1 → *I telephoned you*
2 "I want that you ...", "I'd like that you ..." is German construction. In English we have a different one: → *I want you to ...* or *I'd like you to ...*, here: *I'd like the doctor to see me*
3 → *the same as ...*

An apple a day keeps the doctor away

R: Yes, sir. I'm sorry. Could you fill out this form for our records?
E: No problem. Well! Why do you want to know whether I had sex?
R: I beg your pardon? Oh I see. No, we need to say whether you're male or female.
E: Clear![4] Should I fill the form by myself[5], or will you help me?
R: I can help you, sir, if you've got problems...

(*In the doctor's room*)
D: Now, sir, where's the problem?
E: Well, there gives[6] a sharp pain like a knife in my stomach.
D: Have you eaten anything that might have disagreed with you?
E: Yes, two or three days ago I had your famous fish and chips. They were probably bad.
D: Fish and chips? Not much can go wrong there.
E: I had a doubled[7] portion, something what[8] I don't normally do.
D: Well, I'm not surprised you feel a bit sick. Okay, let's check you out ...

(*Two hours later with Conchita*)
C: ... and what did he say next?
E: I complained about the food for fifteen minutes. And then he told me the whole problem is[9] something other[10]. He wanted to know, had I done[9] any sport.
C: Well, and what did you say?
E: I told that[11] we had visited a gymnasium and had done all-round training to lose weight.
C: But that wasn't too stressful. We were only there an hour. We left at seven. Wait a minute, you didn't come with us. What did you do after we left?

....

4 → "*I get what you mean*"
5 → *fill in the form myself.* "Myself, yourself, himself, herself, ourselves, themselves" is for emphasis. "By myself" means "ich allein".
6 → *there is*
7 → *a double portion*
8 → *something that...* Alles, was = everything that; das, was = those things that
9 Problems with Indirect Speech. Should read → "*he told me the whole problem was ...*", "*he wanted to know if I had done any sport*", "*It said we could train ...*"
10 → *something else*
11 → *I told him that...* After "tell" we need an object, somebody you tell the information to.

An apple a day keeps the doctor away

10

E: You know, before I came to England I read a book about all this training. It said we can train[9] muscles as much as we want if we are used to it.

C: And are you used to it? How much did you train before you came to England?

E: Well, with twenty[12] I trained five times a week.

C: Ernst, that was fifteen years ago. What do you do now?

E: Well, I play skittles once a week.

C: That's what I expected! What did the doctor say was wrong with you?

E: He said I've got a, how do you call it[13]?, a break[14] of the stomach. But he doesn't know what caused it.

C: Ernst, do you know what caused it?

[!] Trouble-shoot that English

Wrong	Right
He said that he has the money.	He said that he had the money.
She wanted to know how old was she.	She wanted to know how old she was.

You should be able to say what other people have told you. This is the grammar point "Indirect Speech". Try to memorise the table of "backshifts".

(TIP)

"I see black".
PRESENT

He said he saw black.
PAST

---

12 → *at the age of twenty*
13 → *what do you call it?*
14 → "Break" is normally "Pause". → Bruch = *rupture*

An apple a day keeps the doctor away

"I'm giving you a chance."
PRESENT CONTINUOUS

She said she was giving him a chance.
PAST CONTINUOUS

"We have never believed him."
PRESENT PERFECT

They said we/they had never believed him.
PAST PERFECT

"She will swindle you."
WILL

He said she would swindle you/him.
WOULD

Questions:

"When was he here?"

She wanted to know when he had been there.

"How did you travel?"

They asked him how he had travelled.

Doctor: I have bad news and some very bad news.
Patient: Well, you might as well give me the bad news first.
Doctor: The lab called me with your test results. They said you had 24 hours to live.
Patient: 24 hours! That's awful! What could be worse? What's the very bad news?
Doctor: I've been trying to reach you since yesterday.

Culture-crossing ▷ Keeping healthy in England

In Britain they still have the National Health System. This means working people pay into the system and all the population have a right to use it. You can also be privately insured (I myself have a private medical insurance called PPP. It costs me about DM 200 per month).

If, like Ernst, you need to see a doctor, you should ring a doctor's surgery first and make an appointment. If it's urgent you can go to a surgery and wait as Ernst did. For very serious conditions you may visit a hospital. Regarding payment most countries have an agreement with GB so that

An apple a day keeps the doctor away

the patient doesn't have to pay. Find out first! After the doctor has seen you, he may write out a prescription (not "receipt") for medicine. There's a charge of a few pounds for each prescription. Go to a chemist's to get your pills.

If you need treatment at the dentist (called in Lachnitisches English "toothdoctor"), you'll have to pay.

A tip! Don't be too ill unless you like being coughed at and walking out with more diseases than you came in with. Of course we're referring to the fact that in England (and even maybe in Germany) the poor patient might have to wait for hours with 200 other patients, or in other words "waiting time is inversely proportional to wealth".

A man went for a brain transplant and was offered the choice of two brains – a lawyer's for £10,000 and a politician's for £100,000. "Does that mean the politician's brain is much better than the lawyer's", asked the man. "Not exactly", replied the brain transplant salesman. "The politician's has never been used."

 Now it's your turn

1. You can get a lot of medicines from the chemist's without a prescription

How good at shopping are you? Match up the problem with the medicine.

1. you have sunburn
2. your eyes hurt
3. you have a bad stomach
4. you want to clean a cut
5. your nose is blocked up
6. you have a sore throat
7. you have a headache
8. you've cut your finger

a. Aspirin or Disprin
b. elastoplast
c. Vick inhaler
d. throat lozenges
e. TCP
f. Optrex
g. calamine lotion
h. Alka Seltzer

An apple a day keeps the doctor away

2. Help our Ernst! At the doctor's

Doctor: How do you do? Please take a seat, will you? Now, what's your problem?
Ernst: Oh doctor, it goes me not good.
Doctor: What sort of symptoms have you got?
Ernst: When I stand up mornings I feel me swindlig. Then suddenly at one time have I head pains.
Doctor: Do you feel any loss of control over your arms, for example?
Ernst: Nay, nothing the same. But what I have, that is the throughfall. It comes so quick, I must run like the devil to the pot.
Doctor: You mean you have to go to the toilet?
Ernst: Yes. Probably the beer.
Doctor: What beer?
Ernst: Na, yesterday evening had we a little fire.
Doctor: And how much alcohol did you drink?
Ernst: Certainly not more as ten of your pints.
Doctor: 10 pints? Go away and take three aspirins. Perhaps they will clear your brain.

3. Which of the following sentences is best?

a. Jenny telephones with Ernst every day because she loves him.
Jenny calls Ernst on every day because she loves him.
Jenny telephones Ernst every day because she loves him.

b. Conchita wants Anna to go swimming with her.
Conchita wants that Anna goes swimming with her.
Conchita wants that Anna went swimming with her.

c. It gives several problems to solve if we want to build this house.
There is several problems to solve if we want to build this house.
There are several problems to solve if we want to build this house.

An apple a day keeps the doctor away

4. Can you put this into Indirect Speech?

Conchita: I'm tired of all this beer. I'd prefer a good glass of Portuguese Dao.

Anna: I know what you mean. Does everybody in Portugal drink wine every evening?

Conchita: We're more interested in a good piece of fish. And the fish needs a good white wine to help it swim.

Anna: Well, in Italy we only drink wine with food. These English seem to drink for the taste of the alcohol.

Conchita: Or for the effect!

Picture your idioms!

German	Wrong	Right
Drück auf die Tube!	Press on the tube!	Step on it!
Alles Banane.	All bananas.	Everything o.k.
Du hast es in den falschen Hals gekriegt.	You've got it in the wrong throat.	You took it the wrong way.

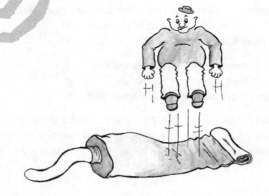

Off to bonny Scotland

11

So they're all off to visit a new town, a new country. This time it's Scotland. But the reality is one we all know. First impressions: nice buildings, a town full of life. Then after an hour or two, depending on your physical condition, it's off to a pub. You're tired and thirsty. And if you're lucky, there are some local specialities to eat. Hmmm!

On the train going to Edinburgh

A = Anna; E = Ernst; J = Jenny; C = Conchita; T = Tourist lady; W = Waitress

A: We'll soon be in Edinburgh. Shall we make a plan of what we're going to do?

E: When we arrive we have to inform ourselves[1] what the most interesting sights are.

A: I'd like to check out the discos.

E: Ah, here's the town. It looks well[2].

J: Do you know it's the first time I've been to Scotland?

C: Pass me the red wine again and then we can celebrate our arrival in Scotland.

E: Caution[3]. You'll be drunken[4] if you drink any more. You know in former times[5] I always wanted to visit the country of haggis, tartan and the Highland Games. It's worth to travel[6] here just for the whisky.

J: You and your wee "dram" of whisky, Ernst. Okay, we're here now. Let's go to the tourist office to get a few ideas.

....

1 → *we should find out*
2 → *good*. After verbs like "get, become, look, taste, smell" we often use the adjective and not the adverb as you might expect:
  The haggis looks awful (not awfully)
  This wine smells bad (not badly)
  It sounds good (not well)
  It tastes horrible (not horribly)
3 → *be careful!*
4 → *drunk*. "Drunken" is only used as an adjective in old songs like "what can we do with a drunken sailor?"
5 → *previously* or *when I was younger*
6 → *it's worth travelling*. We use the Gerund in certain expressions and after prepositions:
  I'm keen on walking ...

Off to bonny Scotland

11

T: You say you've got four days. Well, I'd certainly go up to the Castle. And you could do a day trip to the island of Aran on the west coast.

E: It sounds well², but I wish to see the Grampians, Ben Nevis. I'm keen to walk⁶ in the Scottish Glens.

A: Jesus, it's all a bit physical, isn't it? I'd prefer to visit some typical pubs.

E: Hmmm, Anna, too much alcoholics⁷. You must be careful.

(*One hour later at a restaurant specialising in haggis*):

W: So you'd like haggis prepared with whisky. A good choice if I may say so.

E: (*sticking his knife into the haggis*) Oh, my god! It tastes horribly². But the Scots really eat them. All two minutes⁸ a new haggis arrives for the customers.

J: Be careful! Some of these Scottish specialities are expensive.

E: It's no trouble. I have money enough⁹.

J: Hey, Ernst, you shouldn't say things like that. In England we don't talk about money.

E: I know. You just have it! Let's have another round.

C: The tourist lady said we're only one hour away from Loch Ness. It'd be great to see the monster.

E: I think you won't see¹⁰ any monsters in Loch Ness.

A: Except maybe Ernst, himself. Ha, ha.

E: It has been scientifically proved that there are no monsters in lochs.

J: Oh, Ernst, where's your sense of romance?

E: Romance begins in the evening, not at lunch-time.

A Scotsman was fined for indecent conduct at Edinburgh on Wednesday. According to witnesses the man had continually wiped the perspiration off his forehead with his kilt.

---

7   alcoholic = Alkoholiker → *too much alcohol*
8   → *every two minutes*
9   → *I've got enough money*
10 → In English it's the other way round: *I don't think you'll see*

Off to bonny Scotland

⚠ Trouble-shoot that English

Wrong	Right
It's not worth to worry.	It's not worth worrying.
I'm interested to do a bike ride.	I'm interested in doing a bike ride.

The Gerund (-ing) form can be a bit of a problem. There are some times when we must take this form. Read on to get a feeling for it.

There are some phrases after which we use a Gerund:
It's not worth ...ing
It's no use ...ing

When we have a verb or adjective followed by a preposition like *I am bored with, keen on*, etc., we use a Gerund after it:

*She is keen on visit**ing** foreign countries.*
*It consists of runn**ing**, cycl**ing** and swimm**ing**.*

(TIP)

We also use this Gerund form after certain special verbs.
These include:

risk	imagine
appreciate	put off
avoid	can't stand
dislike	suggest
enjoy	

*I appreciate you(r) help**ing** me last night.*
*She risked los**ing** everything by gambling on the stock market.*

Sex is allowed in Scotland only when Rangers beat Celtic.

Off to bonny Scotland

11 ⌗ Culture-crossing ▷ Scotland

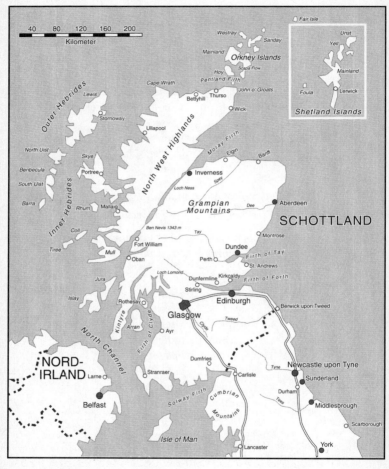

A few facts:
800 islands (130 inhabited)
30,000 lochs
66,628 rivers

5 million people
2/3 of Scotland lies above 120 metres

Off to bonny Scotland

As you see from the information around the map, Scotland is relatively sparsely inhabited. It is also mountainous and is full of lochs and fjords. There's water and rock everywhere. All this means that it is very good for all sorts of outdoor sports.

Hill-walking, rock climbing and mountain climbing
You can walk on the Western Isles, on the Island of Skye, Harris or Lewis. There are many other islands where you can ramble between beautiful lakes and through gentle valleys (glens). Many of the people in these islands still speak the Celtic language. For more professional climbers and walkers the Grampians have difficult dangerous routes. The highest mountain is Ben Nevis.

Winter sports
Because of its terrain and climate Scotland has become a centre for winter sport. You can ski, snowboard and do cross-country skiing. But beware! The weather is changeable. Scots say it can be treacherous.

Fishing
For the more peaceful there is a wealth of various types of fishing. This country is famous for its salmon and trout fishing. There are different trout in each loch. It's not unusual to find men in rubber wellington boots standing in small lochs at 3 o'clock in the night with their fishing rods. Each to his own.

Now it's your turn

1. Help our Ernst! Buying a ticket at the foyer of the cinema

Ernst: Madam, are you tostandig for entry cards?
Clerk: Well, I can sell you a ticket, if that's what you mean.
Ernst: Endly! I will two cards for Titanic.
Clerk: Do you want a seat in the stalls or in the gallery?
Ernst: In the stall? Please excuse, but I am not a horse. Two cards for the hinder rows of the cinema. I carry glass.
Clerk: Oh, I see. Well, I have to tell you that you're not allowed to bring bottles of beer or any other sort of glass into this cinema.
Ernst: Beer bottles? My dame, I mean we are talking past each other ...

Off to bonny Scotland

11

2. Can you put these sentences into English?

a. Meiner Meinung nach lohnt es sich nicht, diese Broschüre ins Englische zu übersetzen.
b. Vorsicht! Wodka trinken kann gefährlich sein.
c. Ich bin sehr scharf darauf, die Wahrheit zu erfahren.

3. Which of the following words in brackets is best for the situation?

a. Walking along the road after the pubs have closed:
Anna: Oh, look at those two fellows staggering around.
Conchita: (Caution, be careful)! You never know what might happen when people are (drunken, drunk).

b. Ernst visits a fitness club:
Trainer: It's really worth (to work out, working out) here every two days.
Ernst: Well, I train (all five days, every five days), but it doesn't do anything for me.
Trainer: As I told you you'll get (healthy, healthily) if you exercise your body more often.

An innkeeper in Scotland mentioned cheerfully at breakfast that the family's ghost had paid him a visit last night. "But he didn't stay very long," he added. "He vanished the moment I asked him for a small gift for the community fund!"

An oyster is a fish that's built like a nut.

Two little fish meet. One asks, "Does a whale have a big nose on it's back?"
"No."
"Oh, Lord. I'm engaged to a submarine."

Off to bonny Scotland

Be idiom-proof!

German	Wrong	Right
Sie stecken unter einer Decke.	They are sticking under a blanket.	They are in league with each other.
Sie ist auf Draht.	She's on wire.	She's on the ball.
Ich werde ihm eins auswischen.	I'll wipe him one out.	I'll get my own back.

Letting your hair down English style

12

We are back in Canterbury, in the pedestrian precinct running through the town, in a pub called the "Dead Duck". By the way, there is a live football match on the TV between Germany and England. Oh dear! Sparks are flying!

➔ Scoring an own goal

B = Barman; **E** = Ernst; **C** = Conchita; **J** = John; **A** = Announcer on TV; **P** = Pub guest

B: So what can I get you?
E: Right, I'll have a lager.
B: Okay, just a minute.
E: Stop! I've done a mistake[1]. I'll have a real ale. Boddingtons. I didn't know you had that.
B: Have you got yourself sorted out yet? Right, it's a Boddys, is it?
E: Yes please!
C: Hey, relax Ernst, we're enjoying ourselves.
E: I am enjoying myself. It makes fun[2] to be here.
J: Ernst, I think you've got to be careful with a few things. Check out the menu or the range of beers before you order. They start pulling the beer immediately here. It's ready after ten seconds.
E: Ten seconds? That's impossible. A friend of me[3] who works in the Heidelberger Schlossquelle told me that a good beer takes six or seven minutes to pour. What's with[4] the froth on top?
J: You mean the head of the beer? They give you that, too. But in most places the customers would kill you if you made them wait seven minutes. It's all a matter of organising your gas pipes.
C: It all tastes the same to me. I think you northern Europeans make a big fuss about beer because you don't understand what a good wine really means. You just want to get drunk.

---

1 ➔ *made a mistake*
2 ➔ *it's good fun to be here*
3 ➔ *a friend of mine, yours, his, hers, ours*
4 ➔ *what about the foam or froth?*

Letting your hair down English style

A: And that's the second goal for England. It doesn't seem to be Germany's day today.
E: Hmmm. That was clearly a foul. That was no goal.
P: What did you say, mate? There was no foul there!
E: Oh, how do you do[5]? I am used to watch[6] football and I mean[7] that this is[8] a foul.
P: A foul? Are you blind?
E: Sir, I must tell you that before ten years[9] I made[10] my licence as a football referee.
P: Good for you, but that was a clear goal!
C: Ernst, let's get another drink. Ernst are you stupid or what?
E: I have made sports[11] for years. What does this fellow know?
C: Are you trying to make trouble? I could make enough comments about Germany if I wanted. I used to live there, you know.
E: You're right. It's really equal[12] in the end.

Boss: Why are you late for work this morning, Ernst?
Ernst: I'm sorry, sir. Normally I dream of my favourite football team and wake up at 7a.m. when the game is over. This morning they had to play extra time.

! Trouble-shoot that English

Wrong	Right
I am used to speak German.	I am used to speaking German.
He's used to travel.	He's used to travelling.

You need to be careful with the structure. If we say "am, is, are + used to" we must follow it with – ing.

---

5 → *Oh hi.* "How do you do" is too formal in this situation.
6 → *I am used to watching*
7 → *I think/ I believe*
8 → *I think that this was a foul* (Indirect Speech)
9 → *ten years ago*
10 → *I did my licence* or *I qualified as ...*
11 → *I've been doing* or *I've done sport*
12 → *It's all the same*

Letting your hair down English style

12

The word "to" is actually a preposition. After a preposition we use a gerund (-ing).

TIP

There is another form which is often confused with "used to –ing". This is "used to" plus Infinitive:

I used to eat haggis. = I ate haggis.
We used to believe our politicians. = We believed our politicians, but now we don't.

The star recruit who had just been transferred for an enormous sum was being interviewed on telly.
"You appear to be earning more money than the prime minister."
"Only fair," said the football star, "I play a lot better than he does."

Culture-crossing ▷ The Brits and their customs

The people of each country have special ways of behaving. You should read about it in advance before you visit a country, or you might make mistakes. Here are a few general questions about the different customs. Compare with your country.

Usual abroad	In your country
Take your shoes off when you enter somebody's home	
Shake hands for the first time you meet someone	
Kiss when you meet a friend you last met six months ago	
Kiss people on both cheeks	
Hold the door open for a woman if you are a man	

Letting your hair down English style

Take a bottle of wine for someone you do not know well
Arrive exactly at the time you were invited

One other thing the English like to do is to make small talk. If you have mastered this rather important technique, you will find it very easy to get into contact with the "little Englanders". And there are many things you can talk about. But for a stranger or a foreigner it's best to begin with the weather. Here's a little help for your small talk about the weather.

On a nice day: "It's a wonderful / beautiful / lovely / marvellous / enchanting day, isn't it?"

On a bad day: "It's awful / terrible / miserable / dreadful / dull / dreary overcast."

For a change in the weather:
"It's changeable, it's clearing up, the sun's peeping through, the wind's dropping."

Of course, when it's hot we start to complain, too:
"It's sticky, sultry, unbearable, boiling, baking, roasting."

  Now it's your turn

1. Are you a small talk/weather specialist?

Match up the types of weather.

1. it's rather sticky
2. it's sweltering
3. it's chilly
4. it's pouring
5. it's drizzling
6. it's clouding over
7. it's clearing up

a. it's hot and wet
b. it's very hot
c. it's raining very fast
d. it's getting better
e. it's getting worse
f. it's raining a little (but it wets you)
g. it's rather cold

Letting your hair down English style

2. At the pub again. Help our Ernst!

Ernst: Hi! How goes it? I had willingly some food for myself and my friends.
Barman: We only do bar snacks in the evening. What can I get you?
Ernst: What for snacks do you sell? A piece of bread with cheese?
Barman: We have hot and cold snacks. A ploughman's lunch would be closest, I guess.
Ernst: No, no, no! You have it in the wrong throat. I don't want lunch, just a little thing in the evening.
Barman: That's what I'm suggesting, a ploughman's lunch.
Ernst: But lunch is at midday. Dinner is in the evening.
Barman: Hey mate, are you pulling my leg?

3. Which of the phrases in brackets fits into the sentences?

a. Ernst: Yes, I (am used to working/used to work) until 10 p.m. every day but now I finish at 6 p.m.
   Conchita: That's what made you rich and boring.
b. Anna: When were you at university, Ernst?
   Ernst: Oh, I finished (before ten years/ten years ago) when I was twenty-eight.
c. Jan: Where did you learn to drive a motorbike like that?
   Ernst: If I (remember/remember me) correctly, I (made/did) my test in 1985.

4. Can you put in the correct tenses of the verb?

The Barmaid (wonder) where the voice came from, before she (see) the little lad in short pants with his nose just reaching the bar.
"Hey, you. I said I (want) a glass of beer and a packet of fags,"(insist) the brat.

The Barmaid saw he (be) a lad of about 13.
"You want to get me in trouble?" she asked.
"(Forget) the sex, just give me the beer and fags," he said.

Letting your hair down English style

Let's catch a few new idioms.

German	Wrong	Right
Eins aufs Dach kriegen.	Get one on the roof.	Get a good talking to.
Ich könnte Bäume ausreißen.	I could pull up trees.	I feel full of beans.
Sie haben wohl zu heiß gebadet.	You've certainly bathed too hot.	You must have been dropped on your head.

Collecting culture

13

Well, when you visit the oldest democracy you have to get into history. England is full of it at every turn and corner. Ernst's language school decided to organise an outflight[1] to the beginning of it all – Battle, where the Battle of Hastings took place in 1066, William the Conqueror conquered and Harold got an arrow in his eye. Later William built an Abbey where Harold had fallen and we're all friends again.

Something about history

The Magna Carta ensured that no free man
could be hanged twice for the same offence.

Columbus said the world was round like an egg.
He was wrong. From the looks of it, it's scrambled.

When Columbus came to America there were no taxes, no debts,
the women did all the work, and the men hunted and fished all day.
How did Columbus expect to improve on a system like that?

Ernst in the High Street, Battle

E = Ernst; **A** = Anna; **C** = Conchita

E: Right. We go to the end of the road and there's the abbey that William built. Yes, there it is. Ah, you my goodies[2]. It's older as[3] I thought.
A: It's very impressive. Actually the whole town is very old.
E: And very large. It surprises me that they can afford to keep it open. It can't be rentable[4].

---

1 → *excursion* or *trip*
2 → *oh my goodness* or *oh my God*
3 Vergleichsform: → *older than*
4 rentable = (ver)mietbar → rentabel = *viable*

Collecting culture

C: Perhaps the tourists have to pay to go in. Ernst, what does it say on that sign?

E: It stands[5] on the sign that Senlac Hill is in that direction. Senlac Hill, that's exactly where William and Harold met. Let's go for a walk there.

A: Oh dear, I'm a bit tired for such a long walk.

E: Nonsense. You slept very long[6] this morning. Let's go!

(They walk around the battlefield and arrive back at the library an hour later.)

C: Hey, you guys, I've just found out that there's a model of the village in the next building. Let's have a look.

E: I drink better[7] a short one[8]. I'm breaking together[9]. I can't concentrate myself[10] at the moment.

C: Who's paying for it?

E: Okay, okay, I'll spend[11] you a drink. What do you want?

A: Oh, Ernst, you're so charming. I'll have a Martini.

C: And I'll drink a port.

(They enter the Bull. Some sort of local Sussex folk band is playing. It's very lively)

E: Ah, this is all very cultural. What a good sound. A group with contra[12], violin, drums and a guitar. It's a good mood[13]. Exceptionally[14] I'll have a cigar. Anna, have you fire[15]?

A: Well, some people did say I was a bit of hot stuff.

E: Ha ha! I mean fire for this black weed here. Thank you.

A: Well, I'm really shocked to see you smoking. You're always telling us how much sport you do.

....

5 with writing on signs, in newspapers etc. → *it says*, here: *the sign indicates that ...*
6 lang schlafen/ verschlafen → *oversleep* or *sleep in*
7 → *I'd prefer to drink*
8 → *a short* = einen Schnaps
9 Idiom in English is: *I can't manage any more* or *I'm at the end of my tether*
10 It's not a reflexive in English: → *I can't concentrate* or *I've lost my concentration*
11 → *it's my turn to get you a drink*
12 → *double bass*
13 „Stimmung" is "mood" on a personal level: "Ich bin schlecht gelaunt. Hier → Stimmung in der Umgebung = *here's a good atmosphere*
14 → *as an exception*
15 Idiom in English is: *Do you have a light?*

Collecting culture

13

E: Nobody is perfect and when I hear[16] music I like to ignite[17] one.
C: What type of music do you normally listen to, Ernst?
E: Folk, jazz and some rock. It hangs from my mood up[18]. This is really great and it's Sunday afternoon. (*Fade out*)

(*It's six in the evening. The three friends are searching for a bed & breakfast.*)

E: I've found a great place. It's called the Old School Cottage. You'd never find it. It's not on the main road. You go through an alley into a garden and there it is. A cottage out of the sixteenth century[19].
C: What does it cost? I'm not too rich at the moment.
E: They have a little prospect[20] where the price of overnight accommodation is £40. And there's an open fire and a heavenly bed[21].
A: All beds are heavenly. What do you mean?
E: It's a bed with a roof and four columns, one at each corner.
C: Oh, Ernst has found a four-poster bed.
E: Yes, I'll sleep like a king.
A: What's the address? I might try a bed & breakfast there myself later.
E: It's the Old School Cottage, 66a High Street, Battle. It's run by a couple who have lived in Germany so the quality must be good.
C: Shut up, my dear Ernst.

❗ Trouble-shoot that English

Wrong	Right
He is richer as me.	He is richer than me (than I am).
They are independenter as our firm.	They are more independent than our firm.

---

16 → Musik hören = *listen to music*
17 → *light one up*
18 → *it depends on my mood*
19 → *a sixteenth-century cottage*
20 → prospect = Aussicht → Prospekt = *brochure*
21 → *four-poster bed*

Collecting culture

We sometimes have some trouble comparing one thing with another.
Here you find two different ways to help you do this.

> **TIP**
>
> We can make comparisons by adding "-er" to the adjective
> followed by "than".
>
> *I am bigger than you.*
>
> When the adjective has three syllables or more we cannot add "-er"
> to the end. It would make the word too long. Here we simply place
> "more" in front of the adjective.
>
> *Annette is more intelligent than René.*
>
> There is another way to make comparisons:
> This form is "as + adjective + as".
>
> *She is just as accurate as you are.*
> *The examinations are as difficult as I expected.*

A father and son were posing for a picture
to mark the son's graduation from university.
"Stand closer," said the photographer
to the father, "and put your hand on his shoulder."
"It would be more appropriate,
if he put his hand in my pocket," replied the father.

Collecting culture

13 ▦ Culture-crossing ▷ The English heritage

What's English heritage? Well, it extends from the real ales through games of cricket and rugby to strawberries at Wimbledon.

But don't forget those big old castles with a thousand years of history behind them. For example, the lovely market town of Newark in Nottinghamshire. Nottingham? Ha ha! That's where Robin Hood met that medieval bull[22], the Sheriff of Nottingham.

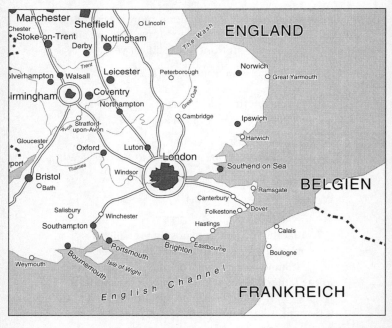

In the south east of England we could mention Hastings and the Battle of Hastings. It was in 1066 when probably the most important battle in English history took place. That's when the Norman French invaded England and poor old Harold, the Saxon got an arrow in his eye.

---

22 German Bulle = Polizist ➜ *cop*

Collecting culture

➕ Now it's your turn

1. Since food is an important cultural item, can you match up the food and the names?

1. steak and kidney pie
2. Cornish pastry
3. bangers and mash
4. shepherd's pie
5. ploughman's lunch

a. meat and vegetable in pastry
b. meat baked under pastry
c. cheese, pickles and bread
d. minced meat covered with mashed potato
e. sausages with potatoes

2. Find the mistakes

Ernst: I'm learning English for more than three years.
Anna: How did you like your course?
Ernst: It was something strange because I was older as all the other students.
Anna: Were the teachers good?
Ernst: It hangs on what you mean with good. Some were good prepared. Some not. But all in all I enjoyed it.

3. Translate the German into English

Ernst: Can you give me (Feuer)? I'd like to (anzünden) a cigar. By the way Anna, I'm thinking of buying a car over here. Have you got a (Prospekt)?
Anna: Well, I've got one for the Land Rover, the Freelander.
Ernst: (Ich würde lieber) buy a more representative car. Like a Mercedes.
Anna: Well, just be careful when you go round corners if the car's full.

4. What should Ernst say in the following situations?

1. He's standing in front of a sign on the wall together with Anna.
    a. "Anna, what stands on that sign? I'm a bit short-sighted."
    b. "Anna, what does that sign say? I'm a bit short-sighted."
    c. "Anna, what is standing on that sign? I'm a bit short-sighted."

Collecting culture

2. Ernst is late for his course.
  a. "Sorry, Tom, I slept long this morning."
  b. "Sorry, Tom, I overslept this morning."
  c. "Sorry, Tom, I slept in this morning."

3. In the pub Ernst "will jemanden einladen."
  a. "Conchita, I'll spend you a drink."
  b. "Conchita, let me invite you."
  c. "Conchita, it's my turn."

On holiday:
A holiday is something you have for two weeks
that takes fifty to pay for.

Local: Lady! I'd come out of the sea if I were you.
There are a lot of sharks about.
Lady tourist: That's all right. They're only man-eating sharks.

The world famous lawyer was holidaying on an
expensive yacht when he fell overboard into a group
of sharks. They declined to eat him out of professional courtesy.

Collecting culture

Idiom peeping

German	Wrong	Right
Sie ist fremdgegangen.	She went strange.	She two-timed him.
Er hat Haare auf der Zunge.	He has hair on his tongue.	He's a tough cookie.
Mach keinen langen Senf!	Don't make long mustard!	Cut it short!

All good things must come to an end

14

And that's just what is happening in the last chapter of Ernst's magical tour of "little England". Don't worry, though! Our hero is ambitious. He will probably be back on his travels to "better" his English, to learn about foreign manners and culture, and not least to keep his friendship with Jenny on the boil.

This final section is a little different. In all the other chapters we gave you help to identify the false friends and "lachnitisms". Here you see the dialogue with the mistakes built in. (They are all mistakes you have met before). Try to find them yourself. Compare with the corrected dialogue at the end of the key.

At Canterbury East railway station

Conchita = C; Jenny = J; and Ernst = E

C: Well, Ernst, I hope you'll come down to Portugal in summer to see how relaxed life can really be.

E: I certainly will. I'll telephone with you before I book my flight. And I bring Jenny with me, my future woman.

J: Hey, slow down a minute, I've only known you for three weeks. But joking aside, Conchita and me have already discussed it.

C: Yes, and there's plenty of red wine and whisky for you there.

E: I'll be drunken the whole day through.

J: But don't put weight on, Ernst. We want to keep you as fit as a fiddle.

E: Of course. By the way, I controlled my weight this morning and my actual weight is two kilos less as when I arrived. Listen Jenny. I'm having an idea. I heard that you'll have a week's holiday in September. That's right, or? What's about us spending the time together?

J: Oh, that's a surprise. It could be a good idea, but we'll have to plan it well. So you want to come back to England, do you?

E: Yes, you see I've got used to drink this strange beer and eat your English breakfast. Oh look, my train comes. I run better or I'll miss it. I would like that you write to me this week.

J: Don't forget to telephone me when you arrive in Heidelberg.

C: And don't drink too much wine on the train.

All good things must come to an end

E: You're making jokes. I don't drink alcoholics when I'm travelling. I'll be working on my laptop.
C: You mean you're going to work a lot.
E: You've got it in the wrong throat. I've bought a golf simulation. I think you two are doing a mistake when you think "all work and no plays makes Ernst a dull boy" as the English say.
C+J: Cheerio. Keep smiling. See you on your next trip.
E: I will do. Although my name's Lachnit, I like to laugh a lot. They could call me "Lachalot". Make it good, you girls.

*And that dear Reader was the end
of the first of the Lachnit sagas.*

Ernst with Jenny's father.
Ernst: Sir, I'm seeking your daughter's hand. Have you any objection, sir?
Father: None at all. Take the one that's always in my pocket.

Women are still the best opposite sex we have.

A woman never forgets her age – once she's decided what it is.

Women who want to be equal to men have no ambition.

All good things must come to an end

14 Have you "bettered" your English? THE QUIZ

1. Why didn't Ernst have dinner at home on his first day at the school?

2. What is wrong with the following?
   Ernst carried the beers on a blue tablet.

3. "Smoked pate". What do you do with it?
   a) drink it
   b) spread it
   c) eat it with a knife and fork

4. I got very angry about it. What did I do?
   a) bent over backwards
   b) hit the roof
   c) muddled through

5. Anna wanted to visit York, but she didn't know her way around. She ...
   a) lost herself
   b) ran way with herself
   c) got lost

6. What do double yellow lines mean at the side of the road?

7. Correct the following.
   They are learning to drive since two years.

8. What is the name of the three pieces of wood sticking in the ground in cricket?

9. What's the name of the "salary" you get at the end of your working life?

10. Improve on the 'If' sentence.
    If Conchita would have known how expensive England was she would never have gone.

All good things must come to an end

14

11. **Improve Ernst's English.**
    "I want to control the bill".
    "That was a very good goal, or?"

12. Ernst is buying a size 42 shirt and a size 41 pair of shoes. **What should he ask for in England?**

13. **Put in the correct form of the verb:**
    Mick received the following letter from his girlfriend:

> Darling Mick,
>
> I'm so sorry that I (quarrel) with you and (call) off your wedding. I'm terribly sorry for all the horrible bad things I (say) about you and I do (hope) that you (forgive) me. I will try to give you anything you (want). Please (give) me one more chance. I know I said I (leave) you for Tony, saying he (be) a much better man than you, but I never honestly (mean) it. Tony (mean) nothing to me. You Mick are all that I (desire). Please (forgive) me and take me back.
>
> Your ever-loving Alison
>
> P.S. May I take this opportunity to congratulate you on winning such a large amount in the lottery.

14. **Where would you go to**
    a) buy alcohol, groceries etc. after the normal shops are closed?
    b) have yourself checked by a doctor?
    c) train your body beautiful?

15. **Can you name two Scottish specialities?**

All good things must come to an end

16. Find the incorrect English in the following dialogue:
- **E:** Barman, I become a pint of lager and my girlfriend will have orange juice. She's making a diet. She thinks she's too thick.
- **B:** Thank you, sir. That'll be £3.
- **E:** Okay. I thank myself. Goodbye ...

17. Remember the German couple who were in the Irish pub in Cork? Why did they leave cursing the Irish?

18. Which of the following sentences is correct?
- a) Press you the button and wait for the traffic lights to change.
- b) Press the button and could you wait for the traffic lights to change.
- c) Press the button and wait for the traffic lights to change.

19. Correct the following dialogue:
(Ernst meets Amy on the train)
- **E:** Hi, I'm Ernst. What's your name?
- **A:** Just call me Amy. Where are you going?
- **E:** I go to a conference in Berlin. Where are you going?
- **A:** I'm off to a teaching seminar. I'm a teacher.
- **E:** Oh, I see. You're teaching English.

20. Can you translate the following into English?
- a) E: Kann ich dir ein Bier oder ein Glas Wein spendieren?
- b) E: Kannst du mir die Kaffeekanne reichen?
   A: Bitte schön.
- c) Ich bin zu weit geschwommen. Mein Rücken tut mir weh.

21. There's something wrong with the following sentences. Find the mistakes:
(John meets Ernst for the first time at the railway station)
- **J:** Hi, you must be Ernst. My name's John.
- **E:** Hello, I'm called Ernst.
- **J:** How long did your flight take? Was it comfortable?
- **E:** The flight has taken an hour and a half. And it has been very rough. We've had a storm.

All good things must come to an end

22. Two people are talking to each other. They're not listening and are having misunderstandings:
   a) they're talking past each other
   b) they're talking at cross-purposes
   c) they're talking to a dead end

23. Read the following idioms. They're not quite right. Can you correct them?
   a) In for a penny, out for a pound →
   b) He was captured with his trousers down →
   c) Don't beat around the porridge →
   d) She's got birds in the belfry →
   e) He was angry. He hit the ceiling →

24. What would the little "Englanders" say for :
   a) einen neuen Anfang machen
   b) einen Dickkopf haben
   c) er hat sämtliche Beine ausgerissen
   d) sich Hals über Kopf verlieben
   e) wollen Sie mich anmachen?

25. And now a little section to check some of the grammar that Ernst met on his trip to England. The following situations are all jokes. Can you put the words in brackets () in the correct form?
   a) The teacher says, "If any of you have to go to the bathroom, please (raise) two fingers."
      From the back, little Johnny says, "How's that going to stop it?"
   b) A teacher told her friend, "I have one child in class who is impossible. He (be) loud and nasty. He (talk) all the time. And the worst thing of all – he's got a perfect attendance record."
   c) A woman (try) on a dozen pairs of glasses with different lenses. Nothing (seem) right for her. To keep her from (become) unhappy, the eye doctor (say), "Finding the right glasses can be very hard."
      The woman said, "Especially when you're shopping for a friend!"

All good things must come to an end

14

d) In a restaurant:
Customer: Excuse me, but how long you (work) here?
Waitress: About three months, sir.
Customer: Oh, then it couldn't have been you who (take) my order.

e) O'leary (from Ireland) is dying. His wife sits sadly at his side. O'leary says, "Remember, my love, Kelly owes me twenty dollars."
"I (write) it down."
"Finnegan (owe) me thirty dollars."
"I (write) it down."
"Sean Gullivan (owe) us fifty dollars."
"Never fear. I (put) that down on paper."
"I owe John Smith two dollars."
"Oh, just listen to the man. His brain just gone dead on him."

f) Amy: If I (go) up to your room do you promise to be good?
Jan: Why – I promise to be fantastic.

g) Two old men are sitting on a bench in the park. One says, "I just (marry) a beautiful girl of twenty-two. She really loves me. She can't get enough sex. She thinks I (be) a great lover."
"What's so bad about that?"
The first one says, "I can't (remember) where I live."

h) A patient called his doctor in the middle of the worst storm of the year and begged him to come out to the house because his wife (be) ill. The doctor asked him why he (not make) an appointment to come in and see him.
The patient said, "In this weather?"

i) The senior civil servant went to the doctor and complained of (be) unable to sleep.
Doctor: Aren't you used to (sleep) at night?
Civil servant: Yes, I sleep well at night. And I sleep soundly most mornings, too – but I've really got problems (sleep) in the afternoon.

Appendix I

EXTRA IDIOMS

We've shown you a lot of idioms during Ernst's trip to England. But you know as well as we do that there are hundreds of other ones. In this appendix we've selected some for you, which are, in one way or another, interesting.

GERMAN	ENGLISH
alle Brücken hinter sich abbrechen	burn one's boats/bridges
alles auf eine Karte setzen	put all one's eggs in one basket
alles ausplaudern	spill the beans
alles verraten	blow the gaff
auf dem letzten Loch pfeifen	scrape the bottom of the barrel
auf den Kern der Sache kommen	get down to brass tacks
auf frischer Tat ertappen	catch red-handed
auf Komplimente aus sein	fish for compliments
auf Nummer Sicher gehen	play it safe
aufs falsche Pferd setzen	back the wrong horse
aufs Ganze gehen	go the whole hog
aus demselben Holz geschnitzt sein	be a chip off the old block
aus der Patsche helfen	save one's bacon
aus einer Mücke einen Elefanten machen	make a mountain out of a mole hill
aus grobem Holz geschnitzt sein	be thick-skinned
aus sich herausgehen	come out of one's shell
aussehen	look as miserable as sin
auswendig lernen	learn by heart
bis in die Puppen arbeiten	burn the midnight oil
bis zum nächsten Morgen durchfeiern	make a night of it
blau wie ein Veilchen sein	be as pissed as a newt
blinden Alarm schlagen	cry wolf

Appendix I

Dampf dahinter machen	pull your finger out
das Eisen schmieden, solange es heiß ist	strike while the iron is hot
das fünfte Rad am Wagen sein	be the odd man out
das ist chinesisch für mich	it's all Greek to me
das ist doch kein Beinbruch	it's not the end of the world
das Kind beim Namen nennen	call a spade a spade
das Kriegsbeil begraben	bury the hatchet
das Sagen haben	call the shots
den Abgang machen	pop off, snuff it
den Bach hinuntergehen	go down the drain
den Bogen raushaben	know the ropes
den Buckel runterrutschen	someone can get stuffed
den Buckel runterrutschen	someone can take a running jump
den Geist aufgeben	give up the ghost
den Hut herumgehen lassen	pass the hat around
den Kopf über Wasser halten	keep one's head above water
den Schwarzen Peter weitergeben	pass the buck
den Ton angeben	rule the roost
der Gelackmeierte sein	be left holding the baby
der Länge nach hinfallen	fall flat on one's face
die Brötchen verdienen	bring home the bacon
die Bücher frisieren	cook the books
die Katze aus dem Sack lassen	let the cat of the bag
die Meinung frei äußern	speak one's mind freely
die Puppen tanzen lassen	raise hell
die Rechnung bezahlen	foot the bill
die Sache auf die lange Bank schieben	let the grass grow under one's feet
die Sache ausbaden müssen	be left holding the baby
die Sache falsch anpacken	get off on the wrong foot

EXTRA IDIOMS

die Zähne zusammenbeißen	grit one's teeth
du kannst nur eines von beidem tun	you can't eat your cake and have it, too
eigennützige Zwecke verfolgen	have an axe to grind
ein blaues Auge bekommen	get a black eye
ein Kauderwelsch reden	talk double Dutch
ein Kauderwelsch reden	talk gibberish
ein königliches Leben führen	live the life of Riley
ein menschliches Rühren verspüren	feel the call of nature
ein schlimmes Ende nehmen	come to a bad end
ein Sklavenleben führen	lead a dog's life
ein Strohmann sein	be a front man
eine lahme Ente sein	have no pep/go/zip
eine lange Nase machen	thumb one's nose at someone
eine Leiche im Keller haben	have a skeleton in the cupboard
eine Stange Geld kosten	cost a pretty penny
einen in der Krone haben	to be well-oiled
einen Schwips haben	be tipsy
einen Zahn zulegen	get a move on
es verkauft sich wie heiße Semmeln	it sells like hot cakes
es zu weit treiben	overshoot the mark
es zu wild treiben	overstep the mark
etwas als nebensächlich zurückstellen	put something on ice, on the back burner
etwas an die Öffentlichkeit bringen	blow the lid off something
etwas beim Namen nennen	call a spade a spade
etwas mit Ach und Krach schaffen	to get through something by the skin of one's teeth
frei von der Leber reden	speak one's mind

Appendix I

ganz oben auf der Palme	be hopping mad
geschehen ist geschehen	it's no use crying over spilled milk
Glück haben	land on one's feet
häßlich wie die Nacht sein	be as ugly as sin
herumlabern	act the goat
immer mit der Ruhe	keep your shirt on
improvisieren	play by ear
in der Tinte sitzen	be in the soup
in die Röhre gucken	sit in front of the gogglebox
ins Fettnäpfchen treten	put one's foot in it
ins Gras beißen	bite the dust
jeder zahlt für sich (Restaurant etc.)	go Dutch
jemandem alles verderben	cook someone's goose
jemandem aus der Patsche helfen	get someone off the hook
jemandem den Laufpaß geben	send someone packing
jemandem die Haare vom Kopf fressen	eat someone out of house and home
jemandem eine runterhauen	box somebody's ears
jemandem einen Anschiß verpassen	to give someone a bollocking
jemandem eins reinwürgen	give someone a real bollocking
jemandem etwas unter die Nase reiben	rub someone's nose in it
jemandem etwas "verpfeifen"	blow the whistle on
jemanden ins Abseits drängen	to push someone into the cold
jemandem Salz in die Wunde streuen	rub salt in the wound
jemanden "anfahren"	jump down someone's throat
jemanden anschnauzen	bite somebody's head off
jemanden auf die Palme bringen	get someone's goat
jemanden hinters Licht führen	lead someone up the garden path

EXTRA IDIOMS

jemanden in Rage bringen	make someone's blood boil
jemanden kaltstellen	bump someone off
jemanden mit Schimpfnamen belegen	call someone names
jemanden richtig ausnehmen	bleed somebody white
jemanden scharfmachen	turn someone on
jemanden überraschen	catch someone on the hop
jemanden wie einen Idioten behandeln	fuck someone around
jemanden windelweich schlagen	beat the living daylights out of someone
kaum zu Wort kommen	not get a word in (edgeways)
kerngesund sein	be as fit as a fiddle
Kopf und Kragen riskieren	risk one's neck
Köpfe werden rollen	heads will roll
kotzen wie ein Reiher	puke one's guts up
krankmachen	swing the lead
krumme Dinge machen	get up to crooked business
kümmere dich um deine eigenen Dinge	mind your own business
laß doch die Dinge auf dich zukommen	don't cross your bridges before you come to them
leben wie Gott in Frankreich	lead the life of Riley
mit heiler Haut davonkommen	escape with one's life
mit heiler Haut davonkommen	save one's skin
mit jemandem anbändeln	pick a quarrel with someone
mit seinem Latein am Ende sein	be at the end of one's tether
neue Besen kehren gut	new brooms sweep clean
nichts auf den Rippen haben	be nothing but skin and bones
nur Haut und Knochen sein	be all skin and bones
nur noch ein halber Mensch sein	feel like a wet rag

Appendix I

ob dir das nun paßt oder nicht	put that in your pipe and smoke it
Oberwasser haben	get the upper hand
qualmen wie ein Schlot	smoke like a chimney
saufen wie ein Loch	drink like a fish
schlafen wie ein Sack	sleep like a log
Schluß machen	call it a day
schmutzige Wäsche in der Öffentlichkeit waschen	air one's dirty linen in public
sein eigenes Loblied singen	blow one's own trumpet
seine Sorgen im Alkohol ertränken	drown one's troubles/sorrows in drink
seinen Beitrag leisten	pull one's weight
seinen Meister finden	meet one's match
sich den Bauch vollschlagen	stuff one's face
sich die Finger verbrennen	burn one's fingers
sich ein Bein ausreißen	bend over backwards
sich in Luft auflösen	go up in smoke
sich nichts anmerken lassen	keep a stiff upper lip
sich prächtig fühlen	feel like a million dollars
sich tapfer halten	put up a good fight
sich über Wasser halten	keep the wolves from the door
sich zusammenreißen/-raufen	pull one's socks up
sich zuspitzen	come to a head
spar dir deine Worte	save your breath
spekulieren	play the market
strohdumm sein	be as thick as two short planks
übe selbst, was du predigst	practise what you preach
über die Runden kommen	make both ends meet
über jemanden triumphieren	have a laugh on
übers Ohr hauen	sell short
um das einmal klarzustellen	set the record straight

EXTRA IDIOMS

um den heißen Brei herumreden	beat about the bush
um es kurz zu machen	cut a long story short
unter Dach und Fach sein	be in the bag
	be signed and sealed
unter dem Pantoffel stehen	be hen-pecked
unter einer Decke stecken mit	work hand in glove with
vom Regen in die Traufe kommen	jump out of the frying pan into the fire
von der Hand in den Mund leben	live from hand to mouth
vor die Hunde gehen	go to the dogs
vor nichts zurückschrecken	stick at nothing
vor Wut schäumen	foam at the moath
Vorfahrt haben	have the right of way
Vorliebe für Leckereien haben	have a sweet tooth
welche Laus ist ihm über die Leber gelaufen?	what's eating him?
wie drei Tage Regenwetter aussehen	look as miserable as sin
wie ein Scheunendrescher essen	eat like a horse
wissen, wo es langgeht	know the ropes
Wurscht sein	don't give a damn
zu Tode erschrecken	jump out of one's skin
zum alten Eisen gehören	be left on the shelf
zum Umblasen dünn sein	you could knock him down with a feather

Appendix II

THE RIGHT WORD AT THE RIGHT TIME

Even the English themselves have a sort of false friends. These are pairs of words which sound almost alike but have different meanings, or are used in different situations. Below is a list of the most common ones with explanations of their usage and meanings.

Take it easy!

EITHER	OR
affect: means to have an influence on something or somebody.	**effect:** the result or consequence of an action.
René was much affected by what Robert said.	*What kind of effect did it have on her?*
all together: is when a number of things are happening or a number of people are somewhere at the same time.	**altogether:** means entirely or totally. If you are 'in the altogether' then this means that you are naked.
The table tennis team arrived all together in one car.	*I'm not altogether sure that this is true.*
amend: to make changes or alterations to something.	**emend:** has a more limited meaning, covering changes, not necessarily corrections, in a text.
The law department amended the contract.	*The agreement was emended to cover new regulations.*
anyway: a synonym for in any case.	**any way:** you can do it as you like; you have the choice.
I'm going to see Conchita anyway; whether you like it or not.	*You can do it any way you like.*

THE RIGHT WORD AT THE RIGHT TIME

around:
We can look around the corner.

round:
The wheels go round.

assurance:
a formal declaration or promise.

insurance:
A contract with which you ensure that you secure compensation for damage, loss or injury.

We require an assurance from you that you will do your best.

I had to take out a life insurance policy, so that the bank would lend me some money.

assure:
assure is used if you want to promise or guarantee something.

insure:
you can insure your car for damage or theft.

I assure you that this insurance is the best on the market.

You need to insure your property.

ensure:
to make something certain.

insure:
see above

I have ensured that you are fully insured.

billion:
used in British English.
German = Milliarde

a thousand million:
same as a billion. Used in American English.

boat:
a small ship. A ship has rescue boats.

ship:
a large vessel used to transport people or freight.

Last year I bought my first sailing boat.

The ship was the biggest cruise ship built in this century.

Appendix II

carefree:
when you are happy and don't worry then you are carefree.

She has a very carefree nature, she is always smiling.

careless:
you are careless if you are not bothered. Is always used in a negative way.

The new trainers were very careless and never arrived on time for their lessons.

client:
solicitors, accountants, advertising agencies, insurance brokers, etc. have clients.

The solicitor lost an important client.

customer:
Shops have customers.

In our shop we depend on regular customers.

contagious:
a contagious disease is caught by direct physical contact with someone.

Herpes is a very contagious disease.

infectious:
an infectious disease is passed on by air or water.

He had bad flu and is still infectious.

continual:
refers to something that is going on all the time but with interruptions.

continuous:
is going on all the time without interruptions.

councillor:
someone who is a member of a council.

I've worked for Rother Council since 1975.

counsellor:
someone who gives you advice.

Frank works as a legal counsellor for Rover.

THE RIGHT WORD AT THE RIGHT TIME

data is:
data is the plural of datum. Both are used. Americans or those working with computers would probably say 'data is'.
You should pronounce it 'dayta' and not 'datta' or 'dahta'.

data are:
using 'data are' there will be people telling you that you are a pedantic fusspot, and those preferring 'data is' may be referred to as ignorant nits.

defective:
use defective if you want to say that something is not working.

The sensor does not detect the signals if it is defective.

deficient:
something is deficient if an important part is missing.

This device is deficient so we'll have to send it back to the manufacturer.

definite:
something is clear and unambiguous.

Ernst gave me a definite description of his car.

definitive:
when something is final and unconditional it is definitive.

The manufacturer's offer was definitive.

dependant:
a person who depends on another for support.

The number of dependants who need to be supported by the State is constantly rising.

dependent:
something is determined by certain factors or if you cannot do without something (like drugs) you are dependent.

Whether I can continue to employ depends on how many new customers we can obtain in the next months.

despatch:
in some books it is stated that despatch is the correct word to use.

dispatch:
however dispatch is much more common.

Appendix II

disinterested:
a disinterested person is impartial, and doesn't allow himself to be influenced by advantages.

A judge must be disinterested.

uninterested:
when you are bored or not bothered you are uninterested.

You could really see that the notary was uninterested, because he fell asleep during the meeting.

e.g.: (Latin for exempli gratia) meaning for example.

The book was translated into many languages, e.g. French, German, Italian, etc.

i.e. (Latin for id est) short form for that is to say.

The book has only been translated into two languages, i.e. French and English.

emigrant:
there is a small but rather important difference. If you leave your country to live in another you are an emigrant.

immigrant:
when you arrive in the new country you are an immigrant.

enquire:
asking for information.

We need to enquire about the price.

inquire:
more like an investigation to get more details.

The tax office inquired about my turnover.

fewer:
for a number of things.
Another little hint is to use 'fewer' if the word after is plural and 'less' if the word is singular.

There are fewer blue-collar workers than white-collar workers.

less:
for a quantity.

Gammelsbach is less than 30 miles away from Heidelberg.

THE RIGHT WORD AT THE RIGHT TIME

fictitious:
when you make something up or imagine it, then it is fictitious.

The supervisory board found out that the balance sheet was fictitious.

fictional:
is an invented idea and doesn't exist in real life.

He showed us a fictional account of a journey to the moon.

impractical:
someone is impractical if he is not able to do things in an efficient way or if something is not worth being put into practice it is impractical.

The machine is impractical, because more operators are needed than before.

impracticable:
something that does not work, or an idea which cannot be carried out.

This idea is impracticable since I cannot organise this amount of money.

last:
is the final thing of more than two.

The last printing unit turns the sheet.

latter:
is the second of two things.

I own a BMW and a Jaguar, I prefer the latter.

mail:
a letter is mailed in the USA ...

post:
and posted in Great Britain.

practice (noun):
Practice makes perfect.

practise (verb):
I need to practise golf, so that I can reduce my handicap.

This problem does not exist for Americans since both words are written with 'c'.

stationary:
when something does not move it is stationary.

So that I can measure the sheet it needs to be stationary.

stationery:
is writing material and office supplies.

Mark lost his job because he stole stationery from the company.

Appendix III

Chapter 1

1. E: Hello, Ernst Lachnit speaking. Could you speak up, please? I can't hear what you're saying.
   E: Yes, I also think we've got a bad connection. I'd like to enrol in your English course in July.
   E: Yes, I do. That's why I'm phoning. Could you send me a form and I'll fill it out?
   E: Could you send it as soon as possible? By fax. I'd like to begin on July 10.
   E: Thank you very much. Bye!

2. a) I attended grammar school / high school for thirteen years and then I became a policeman.
   b) I succeeded in getting a place on a language course.
   c) I have the pleasure of reading this book to improve my English.

3. a) Decide what your level of English is and tick (✓) the box
   b) Don't send off the registration form until you've signed it.
   c) I've eaten too much today. I feel as fat as hell.
   d) All beer in England is warm? I didn't want to say that.

4. 1. c
   2. Scotland, Ireland, Isle of Man, Wales
   3. c
   4. b
   5. c (some may go up to £ 6 or £ 7)
   6. b
   7. c
   8. a, d

Chapter 2

1. E: Waiter, waiter! I'd like to speak to the cook.
   E: I certainly did. This steak and kidney pie is as hard as rock. And it tastes horrible!
   E: But why didn't you serve them until now?

KEY TO THE EXERCISES

2. "Come quickly! Oh, please come quickly," she cried.
   The manager dressed and rushed up to the little old lady's room.
   She was looking through the window and pointing.
   "But madam," explained the manager, "the man is only preparing for bed."
   "Stand on the drawers."

3. a) How much luggage do you have, sir?
   b) I overlooked the fact that my bank card was out of date.
   c) The police have stopped us. Now we're in a real mess.

4. a) I'd like to invite you / treat you to a beer.
   b) Jim: Could you pass me the ketchup, please?
      Ann: Here you are.
   c) Ann: My legs are aching/hurting. I jogged for more than an hour.
      Mother: Well, you shouldn't exaggerate.

Chapter 3

1. I'd like to buy a novel, please.
   Actually I haven't. I was hoping you might suggest something that I could read.
   It's all the same to me. I've got my car outside the door.

2. decided • called • had managed • told • had married • has never been • had to/have had to • were • gritted • rolled • got

3. a) Hi, my name's Amy Fandango. I'm your new teacher.
   b) I'm very impressed with this meal. Could I meet the chef?

Chapter 4

1. Hi miss, could I have a beer, please?
   Yes, I am. I'm thirsty. Could you pull me a draught beer, please?
   For god's sake / for heaven's sake. I'd like a draught lager.
   Closing time? I thought this was a democracy.

Appendix III

2. loved • decided • went • insisted • paid • arranged • How do you like • was

3. a) I explained the problem to him before he tried.
   b) recipe
   c) exaggerate

4. a) Look at this here! It's (written) on page fifteen.
   b) At the chemist's: Could you give me a receipt for the medicine?
   c) In my opinion we should all stop eating meat.

Chapter 5

1. Excuse me, miss. I'm starving. (I'm dying of hunger.) I've been waiting a really long time. Could you give me a menu, please?
   That's good for your profit, but I'd really like to order. Today I fancy/feel like fish.
   The fish sounds good, but I don't want chips. I'd prefer potatoes.
   Of course, but I don't want chips. Have you any pommes frites?

2. a) was addressing • starts • said • are going
   b) was interviewing • are you expecting • replied • said • I'll give • said • it will be

3. a) Canterbury is near Dover.
   b) I was sitting on the London train when I met Amy.
   c) 1. This pub is built completely of wood.
   2. Yesterday evening I ate (had) pork chop with peas and potatoes.
   3. Kathy: Ernst, you know it's your round. You have to invite us to a drink.
   Ernst: That's okay. The mark is very strong.
   Kathy: Well, at least it used to be strong.

KEY TO THE EXERCISES

4. Unfair exercise:

ribs	£ 5.25
burger	£ 3.95
fish & chips	£ 4.95
steak	£ 8.50
garlic bread	£ 1.75
chicken	£ 5.25

Chapter 6

1. Excuse me, sir. I'm trying to find a restaurant called The Blue Boar. Do you know where it is?
   If I remember correctly, along this road, turn right at the end, over the bridge, first left.
   Thanks for asking. It's okay. I'll be going now. Cheerio.

2. were • have given • was • looked • has • seemed • has really been getting / has got • has • have • stirs • is

3. a) I'll buy a bottle of champagne. Money is no object.
   b) Perhaps he's got lost.
   c) Anna wants to try to save some money.

4. a) Conchita has never driven a car.
   b) Anna has been driving for four years.
   c) Ernst is a really friendly person.
   d) The new government has been in office since 1998.

Chapter 7

1. Hi, my name's Ernst Lachnit. I've heard that it costs me £9 for a round of golf.
   Well, it's Monday today. I would like to have played the day after tomorrow, in the middle of the week.
   Yes, that's right, Wednesday, as I said. There are two of us.
   No, not two what! Two players. What else do you expect?
   (to himself) That was difficult enough / That was hard going.

Appendix III

2. buy • called • (had) collected • cures • look • am • turned

3. a) What is the tastiest kind of English beer?
   b) I missed a lot of what you were saying.
   c) That's very interesting! But what about taxes?

4. a) Ernst: Hi, Conchita, I'll come and visit you tomorrow. Perhaps we could go swimming together.
   b) I think I'm in the minority here. / I think I'm alone in my opinion.
   c) That's absolutely right. You've hit the bull's eye.

Chapter 8

1. Two tickets for the show at five o'clock, please.
   Are you hard of hearing? Two tickets for Total Recall.
   That's right. And there's something else. I've got a sweet tooth.
   (I could do with something sweet.) You've got to spoil yourself sometimes.
   I certainly would. / Well, didn't I say that? You're sleeping on the job.

2. a) are • are
   b) were

3. a) I pay DM 600 for my rent every month.
   b) If God had wanted man to fly, he would have created him with wings.

Chapter 9

1. Excuse me, I've seen a pair of trousers in the shop window. I'd like to try them on.
   I don't know my size according to the English system. Do you have a tape measure?
   Have you got a changing room?

KEY TO THE EXERCISES

2. hasn't it? • can't you? • doesn't it? • isn't it?

3. doesn't he? • won't you? • oughtn't he? (didn't he?) • should he? • aren't I ? • didn't she?

4. 1. d   2. f   3. j   4. a   5. c
     6. e   7. i   8 g   9 b   10. h

Chapter 10

1. 1. g   2. f   3. h   4. e
     5. c   6. d   7. a   8. b

2. Oh doctor, I don't feel well.
When I get up in the morning I feel giddy. Then suddenly I get a headache.
No, nothing like that. But I do have diarrhoea. It comes on so quickly, I really have to run.
Yes. It could have been the beer.
Well, last night we had a bit of a celebration.
Well, more or less ten pints.

3. a) Jenny telephones Ernst every day because she loves him.
    b) Conchita wants Anna to go swimming with her.
    c) There are several problems to solve if we want to build this house.

4. Conchita said she was tired of all that beer. She'd prefer a good glass of Dao. Anna agreed that she knew what Conchita meant. She asked if everybody drank wine in Portugal every evening. Conchita informed her that they were more interested in a good piece of fish. She added that the fish needed a good white wine to help it swim. Anna remarked that in Italy they only drank wine with food. She thought that the English seemed to drink just for the taste of the alcohol. Conchita made a joke saying it was just for the effect.

Appendix III

Chapter 11

1. Excuse me miss, do we buy tickets here?
   At last! I'd like two tickets for Titanic.
   In the stalls? Excuse me, but I'm not a horse. Two tickets for the back row of the cinema. I wear glasses.
   Bottles of beer? My dear lady, I think we're talking at cross purposes ...

2. a) In my opinion it's not worth translating this brochure into English.
   b) Be careful! Drinking vodka can be dangerous.
   c) I'm really keen on knowing the truth.

3. a) Be careful! • drunk
   b) working out • every five days • healthy

Chapter 12

1. 1. a   2. b   3. g   4. c   5. f
   6. e   7. d

2. Hi, how are things? I would really like some food for me and my friends.
   What snacks have you got? A cheese sandwich?
   Oh dear, no! You've misunderstood. I don't want lunch, just something small for the evening.
   But lunch is at midday. You have dinner in the evening.

3. a) used to work
   b) ten years ago
   c) remember • did

4. was wondering • saw • want • insisted • was • forget

KEY TO THE EXERCISES

Chapter 13

1. 1. b   2. a   3. e   4. d   5. c

2. I've been learning English for more than three years.
It was a bit strange because I was older than all the other students.
It depends what you mean by good. Some were well prepared, some weren't. But all in all I enjoyed it.

3. a light • light up • brochure • I'd prefer to

4. 1. b   2. b   3. c

Chapter 14

C: Well, Ernst, I hope you'll come down to Portugal in summer to see how relaxed life can really be.

E: I certainly will. I'll telephone *you* before I book my flight. And *I'll* bring Jenny, my future *wife*.

J: Hey, slow down a minute, I've only known you for three weeks. But joking aside, Conchita and I have already discussed it.

C: Yes, and there's plenty of red wine and whisky for you there.

E: I'll be *drunk* all day.

J: But don't put on weight, Ernst. We want to keep you as fit as a fiddle.

E: Of course. By the way, I *checked* my weight this morning and my *current* weight is two kilos less *than* when I arrived. Listen Jenny. *I have* an idea. I heard that you'll have a week's holiday in September. That's right, *isn't it*? *What* about us spending the time together?

J: Oh, that's a surprise. It could be a good idea, but we'll have to plan it well. So you want to come back to England, do you?

E: Yes, you see I've got used to *drinking* this strange beer and *eating* your English breakfast. Oh look, my train *is coming*. *I'd better run* or I'll miss it. I would *like you* to write to me this week.

J: Don't forget to telephone me when you arrive in Heidelberg.

C: And don't drink too much wine on the train.

Appendix III

E: You're *joking*. I don't drink *alcohol* when I'm travelling. I'll be working on my laptop.

C: You mean you're going to work a lot.

E: You've got it *wrong*. I've bought a golf simulation. I think you two are *making* a mistake when you think "all work and no play makes Ernst a dull boy" as the English say.

C+J: Cheerio. Keep smiling. See you on your next trip.

E: I will do. Although my name's Lachnit, I like to laugh a lot. They could call me "Lachalot". *Take care*, you girls.

The quiz

1. Because his fellow students wanted to visit an old pub
2. He carried the beers on a blue tray
3. b
4. b
5. c
6. No parking at any time
7. They have been learning to drive for two years
8. Wickets or stumps
9. Pension
10. If Conchita had known how expensive England was she would never have gone.
11. I want to check the bill
    That was a very good goal, wasn't it?
12. Could I have a size 16 1/2 shirt and a pair of size 7 shoes
13. quarrelled • called • said • hope • forgive • want • give • was leaving • was • meant • means • desire • forgive
14. a) an off-licence
    b) a doctor's surgery
    c) a gymnasium
15. Whisky and haggis
16. I'll have a pint • I'd like a pint • she's on a diet • she thinks she's too fat • Okay, thank you

KEY TO THE EXERCISES

17. They left because nobody came to their table, so they thought it was bad service, perhaps because they were foreigners.

18. c

19. Hi, my name is Ernst.
I'm going to a conference in Berlin.
Oh, I see. You teach English.

20. a) Can I treat you to a beer or a glass of wine?
    b) Could you pass me the coffee pot?
       Anna: Here you are!
    c) I swam too far. My back is hurting.

21. Hello, my name's Ernst.
The flight took an hour. It was very rough. We had a storm.

22. b

23. a) in for a pound
    b) he was caught with ...
    c) ... around the bush
    d) she's got bats in her belfry
    e) he hit the roof

24. a) turn over a new leaf
    b) be pig-headed
    c) he bent over backwards
    d) fall head over heels in love
    e) Are you trying to chat me up?

25. a) raise
    b) is • talks
    c) tried • seemed • becoming • said
    d) have you worked or have you been working? • took
    e) I'll write. owes • I'll write • owes • I'll put that down
    f) I go
    g) I've just married • I am • remember
    h) was • didn't make
    i) being • sleeping • to sleep

Appendix IV

abbey	Abtei
accident	Unfall
accidentally	zufälligerweise
accommodation	Unterkunft
accompany	begleiten
accurate	genau / akkurat
aches	Schmerzen
act	Akte
actual	tatsächlich
address	ansprechen
advice	Ratschlag
afford	sich leisten
agree	einer Meinung sein / übereinstimmen
alley	Gasse
allocate	zuordnen
anyway	auf jeden Fall
appropriate	geeignet
approx.	ungefähr
arise	sich ergeben/entstehen
arrow	Pfeil
as a rule of thumb	über den Daumen gepeilt
astonished	erstaunt
attitude	Einstellung
authority	Behörde
awful	schrecklich/furchtbar
baking	backen
bangers	Würstchen
bargain	ein gutes Geschäft
barrage balloon	Sperrballon
barrel	Faß
basically	im Grunde
bat	Fledermaus
batter	(Bier-)Teig
battlefield	Schlachtfeld
bearded	bärtig
beat	schlagen
behaviour patterns	Verhaltensmuster

VOCABULARY

belfry	Kirchturm
beware	Vorsicht
bitter	stark gehopftes Bier
blame	beschuldigen
bloody awful	verdammt schlecht
boarding house	Pension
boil	kochen
bona fide	echt
bonny	schön
book	buchen, reservieren
border	Grenze
borrow	leihen
bowl	Kugelspiel auf Rasenplätzen
brag	prahlen, angeben
brainy	intelligent, gescheit
brat	Gör
breaded	paniert
briefing	Anweisungen
browse	schmökern (in einem Buch)
bunch of roses	Rosenstrauß
by Jove	Donnerwetter
case	Fall
cash	Bargeld
cash desk	Kasse
changing room	Umkleidekabine
chat someone up	jemanden anmachen
construction	Bau
celebrate	feiern
century	Jahrhundert
changeable	wechselbar
charge	belasten
charming	charmant
cheek	Frechheit
circumstances	Umstand
clear up	aufklären
clouts	Unterhose
cod	Kabeljau

Appendix IV

coincidence	Zufall
column	Säule
comparison	Vergleich
competition	Wettbewerb
complain	sich beklagen
condition	Bedingung
confuse	verwirren
conquer	erobern
continuous form	Verlaufsform
corner	Ecke
cough	husten
counter	Theke
courtesy	Höflichkeit
cranberry	Preiselbeere
creep	kriechen
crisp	knackig
crunch	mampfen
crunchy	knusprig
cure	heilen
currency	Währung
curse	fluchen
customer	Kunde
customs	Gebräuche, Zoll
cutlet	Schnitzel
debt	Schuld
decide	entscheiden
decision-makers	Entscheidungsträger
deep-fried	fritiert
definite action	bestimmte Handlung
definite articles	bestimmte Artikel
delicious	lecker
depend	abhängig von
design	Entwurf
destination	Reiseziel
dill	Dill
disappear	verschwinden
disease	Seuche

VOCABULARY

dish	Essen, Gericht
double yellow lines	absolutes Halteverbot
drift off	abtreiben
drag	schleppen
dram	Schluck
drawer	Schublade
drawers	Unterhose
dreary	langweilig
dresser	Frisierkommode
drums	Trommel
economical	wirtschaftlich
eloquent	redegewandt
embarrass	in Verlegenheit bringen
employee	Angestellte
enclosed	beigefügt
endure	aushalten
enduring	andauernd
enrolment form	Anmeldeformular
ensure	versichern
entertainment	Unterhaltung
envelope	Umschlag
equipment	Ausrüstung
eternal	ewig
eternity	Ewigkeit
everyone to his own	jeder nach seinem Geschmack
evil tongues	böse Zungen
exaggerate	übertreiben
excerpt	Auszug
excursion	Ausflug
executives	Topmanagement
facility	Einrichtung
fag	Glimmstengel
fail	keinen Erfolg haben/mißlingen
filleted	filetieren
fitter	Schlosser
fluent	fließend
folder	Mappe

Appendix IV

fool	Narr, Idiot
force	zwingen
forehead	Stirn
frantic	verzweifelt
fruity	fruchtig
froth	Schaum
gallon	entspricht circa 4 Liter
garlic	Knoblauch
garnish	garnieren
gents	meine Herrschaften
ghouls	Dämon
gift of the gab	gut reden können
goal	Tor / Ziel
gogglebox	Fernseher
goodies	Annehmlichkeiten
goose pimples	Gänsehaut
governor	Umgangssprache für "alter Herr"
graduation	Universitätsabschluß erlangen
grain	Korn
grant	gewähren
grit	Kies
guarantee	Gewährleistung
guess	raten
gut	Wampe
habit	Gewohnheit
haddock	Schellfisch
haggis	eine Art schottischer Saumagen
half-masticated food	halb vorgekautes Essen
handsome	gut aussehend (Männer)
hassle	Mühe
hastily	hastig
height	Höhe
herbs	Kräuter
heritage	Erbgut
hiccups	Schluckauf
hi-jack	entführen
hint	Hinweis

VOCABULARY

hiss	zischen
hose	Schlauch
host	Gastgeber
hunt	jagen
ignite	entzünden/zünden
immediately	sofort
impregnate	schwängern
impressed	beeindruckt
impressive	imponierend
in accordance with	entsprechend/gemäß
indecent	unanständig
indecent conduct	unanständiges Benehmen
infinitive	Grundform
insist	bestehen auf
inspection	Untersuchung
instruction	Anweisung
insurance	Versicherung
insure	versichern
intention	Absicht
intermediate	Mittelstufe
interview	Interview
introduce oneself	sich vorstellen
invent	erfinden
investigator	Ermittler
issue	ausgeben
just this time	aber nur diesmal
keep her company	ihr Gesellschaft leisten
key	Schlüssel
kilt	Schottenrock
knockdown price	Schleuderpreis
lads	die Jungs
lawyer	Rechtsanwalt
leisure time	Freizeit
level	Niveau
library	Bibliothek
limit	Grenze
linger	verweilen

Appendix IV

liquid	Flüssigkeit
magnificent	herrlich
map	Landkarte
marks	Schulnoten
mash	Kartoffelpüree
masticated	zerkauen
match	zuordnen
matches	Streichhölzer
mate	Freund, Junge, Kumpel
medical insurance	Krankenversicherung
menu	Speisekarte
mess	Durcheinander
message	Botschaft
mileage	Kilometerstand
minced meat	Hackfleisch
miraculous	wunderbar
missing	vermißt/gesucht
misunderstanding	Mißverständnis
monitor	überwachen
mortgage	Hypothek
muddle through	durchwursteln
multitude	Vielfalt
mushy	matschig
nightmare	Alptraum
no debts	keine Schulden
nut	hier: der Bekloppte
nutty	bekloppt
oblong	länglich
odd	gelegentlich
off-licences	kleine Geschäfte, die nicht an die Ladenöffnungszeiten gebunden sind
offence	Straftat
ordinary	gewöhnlich
originate	entstehen
overcast	bewölkt
owner occupier	Eigenheimbesitzer
pain	Schmerz

VOCABULARY

parrot	Papagei
participant	Teilnehmer
pastime	Hobby
paté	Pastete
pedestrian precinct	Fußgängerzone
peep	neugierig lugen
pension	Rente
perform	ausführen
permit	erlauben
perspiration	Schweiß
pet	Haustier
petty cash box	Kasse
pickles	Gewürzgurke
pie	Pastete
pig-headed	dickköpfig
pint	ca. ein halber Liter
pipe	Pfeife, Rohr
placement test	Einstellungstest
plaice	Scholle
pleasure	Vergnügen
poached	dünsten/wildern
polite	höflich
population	Bevölkerung
porridge	Haferbrei
pour	gießen
practise	üben
prefer	bevorzugen
pregnant	schwanger
preposition	Verhältniswort
prescription	Rezept
pretty	hübsch
presume	vermuten
progressive	Verlaufsform
proof	Beweis
prove	beweisen
pull yourself together	reiß dich zusammen
purpose	Zweck

Appendix IV

pursue	verfolgen, ausüben
push	drücken
queue	Menschenschlange
quote	Zitat
rake	Rechen
ramble	herumstreifen
range	Reihe, Auswahl
records	Unterlagen
recommend	empfehlen
register	einschreiben/anmelden
registration	Anmeldung
registration form	Anmeldeformular
regularly	regelmäßig
reinforce	verstärken
reliable	zuverlässig
remind	sich erinnern an
rent	Miete
reply	erwidern
roasting	braten
role-play	Rollenspiel
roof	Dach
rot	verfaulen
rotten	verfault
rough	rauh, grob, hart
round off	abrunden
rust	Rost
salmon	Lachs
schedule	Zeitplan
score	erzielen
scrambled eggs	Rühreier
selection	Auswahl
send somebody off with a flea in his ear	jemanden wie einen begossenen Pudel abziehen lassen
sense	Sinn
sentence	Satz
serve	dienen
shake	zittern

VOCABULARY

shallow	flach
shark	Hai
shot	Schuß
shriek	schreien
sick	krank
side street	Gasse
sight	Sehenswürdigkeit
sign	Schilder
size	Größe
skilful	geschickt
skin	häuten
skittles	Kegel
slice	in Scheiben schneiden
smooth	glatt
sniff	schnuppern
sob	Schluchzen
soggy	durchnäßt / matschig
sort out	sortieren
sound	Klang
source	Quelle
sparsely	spärlich
spear	Speer
spectator	Zuschauer
spice up	würzen
spicy	gewürzt
spike	einen Schuß Alkohol in ein Getränk geben
spoon	Löffel
stagger	schwanken, torkeln
stall	Stall
state	Zustand
sternly	streng
stew	Eintopf
stick	Holzstiel
sticky	klebrig
stir	rühren
storage	Lager

Appendix IV

street guide	Sraßenführer
stretch	über etwas hinweglangen
struggling	abmühen
stuff	Zeugs
successful	erfolgreich
suit	passen
sultry	schwül
summon	herzitieren
suppose	annehmen
surgery	Arztpraxis
swallow	verschlucken
sway	schwanken
sweat	schweißen
swindle	Betrug
syllable	Silbe
tablet	Pille
tabloid	Boulevardzeitung
talk at cross-purposes	aneinander vorbeireden
talkative	gesprächig
taste	schmecken
tasteless	geschmacklos
taxes	Steuer
telly	TV, Fernseher
tend	neigen zu ...
thin as a rake	dünn wie eine Bohnenstange
tidy up	aufräumen
till	Kasse
tip	Hinweis
timetable	Stundenplan
tortoise	Schildkröte
totter	wanken
transplant	transplantieren
treacherous	hinterhältig
trout	Forelle
treat	behandeln
triangle	Dreieck
trip	Reise

VOCABULARY

troublesome	schwierig
trust	vertrauen
tube	Rohr
turkey	Truthahn
turn	drehen
turnover	Umsatz
tutor	Lehrer
twins	Zwillinge
unbearable	unausstehlich
uncomfortable	unbequem
undercooked	nicht gar
urgent	dringend
useless	nutzlos
vocabulary	Wortschatz
waddle	watscheln
wave	Welle
wealth	Reichtum
wee	klein (schottische Umgangssprache)
weed	Unkraut
weight	Gewicht
wheel	Rad
whole	ganz
wickets	Dreistab (Kricket)
wipe	wischen
wobble-bottom	Wackelhintern
wonder	Wunder
yawn	gähnen
yeast	Hefe

Com-be-nations

Communication between nations

Personal Executive Language Consultants

Improve your technical English
with the authors of this book.

A language seminar
customized to your company.

Contact

Dr. René Bosewitz
Com-be-nations
Communication between nations

Czernyring 22/12
69115 Heidelberg
Tel.: 0 62 21 2 75 90
Fax 2 75 13